P9-APJ-282

Everything You Always Wanted to Know About **TAXES** but Didn't Know How to Ask

Everything You Always Wanted to Know About

TAXES

but Didn't Know How to Ask

Michael Savage

The Dial Press   New York

Published by
The Dial Press
1 Dag Hammarskjold Plaza
New York, New York 10017

Manufactured in the United States of America

First printing

Library of Congress Cataloging in Publication Data

Savage, Michael, 1946–
    Everything you always wanted to know about taxes
but didn't know how to ask.

    Includes index.
    1. Income tax—United States—Law. 2. Tax
planning—United States. I. Title.
KF6369.3.S27   343′.73′052   78–24306
ISBN 0–8037–2320–2

To Mirtha

Contents

Preface

Have you ever wondered why it is sometimes cheaper to "live in sin" than to get married?

Have you ever asked why alimony to your ex-wife may or may not be deductible depending on how you pay it?

When is a travel expense not a travel expense? When is income *not* income?

What did Congress have in mind when it mapped out the medical-expense deductions that read like "Take two from column one and one from column two and then pass 'go' and return to square one"?

How can you save taxes on the "declining" value of property while its market value is actually increasing?

If you were to ask three IRS agents a moderately complex tax question, you could very well get three different answers. "Yes," "No," and "We don't answer questions like that. Ask your tax advisor." Your tax advisor might readily come up with the answer. Or he might think about it for a while, read a few books, and consult his partners, only to decide that there is no certain answer. "We'll have to ask the IRS," he might say. Once it is established that nobody knows the answer because there are conflicting answers, the question might be posed to Congress, which is like asking the fox to feed the chickens. Two years later, Congress would supply an answer which made no sense at all, and by then you would have forgotten the question anyway.

Exaggerations? Not if you've been there.

If the federal tax law is so complex that even experts can be puzzled by relatively uncomplicated questions, how can you, the average taxpayer, understand it? The outrageous fact is that no one expects you to understand it. "Pay and don't ask" is the attitude that prevails. Congressmen, lawyers, accountants, and pollsters all agree that the overwhelming majority of Americans have little, if any, understanding of the United States income-tax system.

But you have a *right* to understand—because week by week, month by month, quarter by quarter, year by year, that system takes away your money.

This book will help you to understand the laws that most commonly affect the average taxpayer. (Corporations and individual tycoons are another matter.) We will discuss income, deductions, and credits, and why some people pay so little tax. And business-tax problems you might run into, and tax shelters and how they work. And more. The tax laws are not unbeatable; they are only intimidating. You can understand them and how to tackle them.

The President thinks that the tax laws are a "disgrace to the human race," and he has been calling for major changes; in fact, those changes aren't so major. As we consider each topic we will examine some of the changes. You will see that they are mostly sugar-coating—that they are changes in numbers and percentages, not in substance.

Your problem is not with percentages—except to pay

them. Your problem is with the underlying mass of rules, regulations, instructions, and contradictions, and it is to that that we will direct our fire. Our intention is not to give legal advice, and the book cannot be relied upon as legal advice. A book which gave answers to all tax problems for all people in all situations would just be a rewrite of the tax laws themselves, and no less overbearing. Our intention is to put the tax law in perspective, to make some sense out of that underlying mass so that you can get a handle on it, to help you understand what is going on here, and why.

People are said to be fed up with taxes, and this so-called "tax revolt" may soon extend to federal income taxes. But with federal taxes some people do not seem to understand what they are rebelling against. Polls indicate that the same people who support a broad concept called "tax reform" oppose specific changes which many experts offer as the building blocks of tax reform. This book is not intended to strike a blow for or against tax reform or to further or inhibit any tax rebellion. It may, however, help you decide whether you wish to join the struggle, and on which side.

Everything You Always Wanted to Know About **TAXES** but Didn't Know How to Ask

ONE
In the Beginning There Was Gross Income

It is news to practically no one that the United States Government imposes an "income" tax on citizens and residents. You might think that this state of affairs would have prompted some alert congressman to define the term "income." Nothing so logical happens in Washington. Congress fired shots all around the target. It defined "gross income," "adjusted gross income," "taxable income," "earned income," and "ordinary income," but nowhere in the two thousand pages of the Internal Revenue Code is there a definition of "income." The oversight changes nothing. Your income gets taxed just the same.

In the tax law you start with "gross income." Gross income is Congress's attempt to describe what it means by "income." You might feel the term "gross income" is ill chosen because these days no one's income seems particularly gross—except for purposes of the tax laws. It is from gross income that the government ultimately takes its cut, and so Congress gave the term "gross income" the most comprehensive, all-inclusive definition it could find. Here is what it came up with:

Gross income means all income from whatever source derived.

For the Internal Revenue Code, that is a rather simple definition. In even simpler language: "If you get it, it's income."

Of course there are exceptions. Gross income is not really "all income from whatever source derived." Lawyers write laws and lawyers make money because of exceptions. The tax laws—and all laws—would be quite simple but for the exceptions. We'll talk about the exceptions later. Congress talks about the exceptions later—after it gives you the definition quoted above. But it starts with this voracious definition. It gathers all its marbles before it starts to give them away.

The answer to the question, "What is gross income?" (or, "What do I have to include in income?") is simple. EVERYTHING. Obviously your salary is an item of gross income, as are dividends from your stocks, interest payments on your savings accounts, and money you make when you sell property at a profit. These things are clearly income—they are monies which you get for working hard or for being smart (or, in some cases, both). But suppose you receive money for not doing much of anything. You are divorced, for example, and you receive alimony payments every month. Is that gross income? Of course it is. If you win the lottery that's income too. If your horse comes in—income. Suppose you owe somebody $100, and then one day you rescue him from the sea and he says, "Forget about the $100 you owe me." That is income—$100 of it. Even if you don't save their lives, you have income if your creditors cancel your debts. Even if you let them drown and the debts are never collected, it's income to you.

Suppose you are walking down the street and you find a $1000 bill. That is income; you have to pay taxes on that.

Suppose instead you find a diamond worth $1000. Income. Suppose you find a dull pencil. Income, and well it should be if you're crazy enough to report it to the Internal Revenue Service.

Poker winnings, the umbrella you find in a taxicab, the tools that the plumber forgets in your house and you keep —it's all income, every penny of it.

If you own a hardware store and an electrician fixes a light in your house and says, "Instead of paying me $30, give me a drill from your store," and you do, that is $30 of income to you and $30 of income to him. You are supposed to report that on your 1040 form. Even if you don't own a hardware store but just give him a drill from your house—income to him, income to you.

The rental value of the company suite you live in for free as president of your firm is income to you. So is a portion of the value of the company car you drive, if you use it part of the time for personal reasons. And the money you find in a chair which you got free from Goodwill Industries. Even the money you extort from a kidnapping victim or rob from a bank is income. You may get caught and go to jail if you report it, but you may also go to jail if you don't report it because failing to report income is a crime. That is why mobsters are often indicted on tax-law violations.

You can see that it doesn't matter what form your income takes. It can be cash, stock certificates, services, housing, or a year's supply of cotton candy. If it has value and you get it, it's income. One taxpayer organized a European trip for a tour operator. His reward: a free trip with the tour. Income. The value of the trip was income even if he had a lousy time.

If you have a question as to whether something in particular is income, the answer is, Yes. It's all income.

This is how the tax law starts and there is nothing complicated about it. You don't have to worry about whether something is income and should be included in gross income. *All* income, from *whatever* source derived, is gross income. Everything is included. EVERYTHING. Unless . . .

Unless it's excluded.

The Internal Revenue Code is uncomplicated for about eleven seconds.

Why is everything included if some things are excluded?

It may seem absurd to say that everything is included in gross income when in fact some things are excluded. However, compared to what is coming, it's brilliant. Not only is everything included even though some things are excluded, but in addition some things are "specifically" included. Now why include some things "specifically" if everything is already included anyway (except for the things that are excluded)? Write your congressman. Or go on to the next page.

TWO
Go Back Two Spaces

It helps to know what the Internal Revenue Code looks like. One reason the tax laws are so complicated is that they have to be written down, and the answer to your little tax problem may start on one page, pick up again five hundred pages later, and conclude six hundred pages after that. Life would be simpler if Congress could simply transmit the tax laws to the taxpayers in a flash, or if a picture were worth, say, twenty-three trillion words. Unfortunately, it all has to be written down, page after page, chapter upon chapter. Lest you jump to any conclusions that might deplete the federal treasury, Congress very early says, in effect: In-case-you-read-no-further-everything-is-income. Later on it backs off.

Everything is included; except . . .

Like sculpture, you start with clay or a rock and go from there, chipping away, shaping.

The Internal Revenue Code begins substantively at section 61. (It ends at section 9042.) Sections 1 through

58 are just warm-up. They tell you what the tax rates are for different kinds of people with different incomes (more on that later). They also tell you about tax credits. Tax credits are little items that enable you to reduce your tax liability. They are credits against any tax you might owe if it weren't for the tax credits. Tax credits are mostly for rich people and corporations—so that they won't have to pay much tax. It is noteworthy that the information on how to reduce your tax liability appears toward the beginning of the Code, not toward the end. It is right up front, perhaps so that rich people, whose time is valuable, won't have to struggle through all the rules on tax liability only to discover that they don't have any (more on tax credits later).

The real Code begins at section 61. Section 61 contains the definition of "gross income" quoted back on page 4. However, the definition quoted on page 4 is not the complete definition. Nothing in the tax law is that simple. The definition of gross income actually starts like this:

> Except as otherwise provided in this subtitle, gross income means all income from whatever source derived, including (but not limited to) the following items: . . .

"The following items" include some mentioned earlier: salary, money you make on selling property, dividends, interest, alimony, debt-forgiveness; not to mention rents, royalties, annuities, pensions, and many other items.

After section 61 ("gross income"), the Code goes on (through section 65) to define a few other things, including "adjusted gross income," "taxable income," and "ordinary income." Then, starting with section 71, it lists "Items *Specifically Included* in Gross Income"—items included on top of everything else that is included. That continues through section 84. From section 101 to section 124, the Code lists "Items *Specifically Excluded* from Gross Income." Items not included even though everything is included.

That is how the core of the Code—the part that describes income—looks. Three separate subparts. Gross income in general, items specifically included, and items specifically excluded.

In case you're wondering, there are no sections 66–70, nor 85–100. They simply don't exist. In Washington when things don't exist, we say "It got cut out in Committee" or "It was dropped on the House floor." But sections 66–70 and 85–100 are not lying on the House floor. These sections were purposely left out to enable Congress to add a few things later without having to renumber thousands of sections. Congress knew it would screw up and would have to make changes.

Returning to the definition of "gross income," you can begin to see why we say that everything is included unless it's excluded. That is what the Code says. But the Code is not merely trying to make your life difficult; it is only creating a presumption that everything is income. The Congress is saying, "Don't waste your time wondering whether something is income or arguing about whether it should be income. It *is* income, unless we say otherwise." If you ask the IRS or your lawyer, "Why is that item included in income?" the answer is simply, "Because it's not excluded."

THREE
What Is "Specifically Included" in Gross Income?

It is easy to understand why Congress included every-thing in gross income "except as otherwise provided." It was damn sure that it wanted to include more things than it wanted to exclude. (Remember, congressmen's salaries and expenses are paid from your tax dollars.)

It is also easy to see why Congress specifically ex-cludes certain items from gross income. It goes back to the problem of having to write it all down. Congress wanted to exclude certain items but couldn't do it all at once—in a picture or a flash. So it included everything, "except as otherwise provided," and then it provided otherwise elsewhere.

But why, after including everything except as other-wise provided, did it then *specifically* include some things? The guiding concept here is this: While every-thing is included in income, everything is included in income only once. Something which has already been included in your income cannot be included in your income again, or in someone else's income. The problems begin when there is a question as to when it's included in income, or whose income it's included in. By stating that some things are "specifically" included in income, Congress (at least in most cases) is not deciding *whether* something is income, but *when*, or *to whom*. Everything is income unless it is excluded from income—but some things are income at different times or to different people.

Alimony, for example. The husband earns $25,000 per year and is under a court order, or has executed a separation agreement, to pay $12,500 of it to his former wife. Whose income is the $12,500? He earns it, but under the order or agreement he has no right to it. And how could he afford to pay taxes on all his income when he must give half of it away? Under the tax laws you get taxed only on income which you have a right to receive. And so we have our first item "specifically included" in gross income:

> Section 71. *Alimony and Separate Maintenance Payments.* If a wife is divorced or legally separated from her husband . . . the wife's gross income includes periodic payments . . . received . . . in discharge of a legal obligation . . . imposed on . . . the husband [i.e., alimony].

Under another section of the Code, the husband gets to reduce his income by whatever amount the wife includes in hers under section 71.

You may be thinking that this is a sexist law, and wondering whether alimony payments to a husband are included in his gross income. There is no loophole here. Over a thousand pages later, in section 7701, the Code gets around to explaining that the terms "husband" and "wife" are interchangeable in section 71. Congressmen may be crazy, but they're not stupid.

Alimony, then, is income "specifically included" so that you'll know whose income it is, or when it's income. I will give you another case in a moment, but let me finish with alimony, just to show you how complicated a bunch of congressmen can make a simple thing. Monthly or yearly ("periodic") alimony, we have seen, is income to the wife. If instead of paying alimony periodically the husband agrees or is ordered to pay a single sum all at once or even in a few installments—a "lump-sum settlement"—the amount the wife receives is *not* income to her. Why? There is discernible logic here. The money making up a lump sum will probably come from the husband's savings or other assets and will have already been included in his income and taxed. Also, the wife would end up paying a stiff tax if the lump-sum amount were large, which would mean that the husband would have to pay even more alimony, and congressmen would be unpopular.

The lump-sum rule is different if that single amount is to be paid over a period of more than ten years in approximately equal amounts. Then it is income to the wife as she receives it and the husband gets to reduce his income. (In any one year, the wife may never include in her income, nor the husband deduct from his, more than 10 percent of the principal sum.) If she gets paid over a period of more than ten years, the money is more likely to be coming from the husband's yearly income and so tax liability is shared. Also, the tax on the smaller annual amount won't be so painful to the wife.

There are more variations on these alimony rules. The purpose of all of them is to apportion the tax burden as fairly as possible. Congress doesn't sock the wife with a big tax if she gets a lump sum, but if the money comes from the husband's income, she is responsible for part of the tax. The rules are not perfect, but then neither is the Congress.

Alimony payments should not be confused with payments specifically designated as child support. These amounts are never income to the former spouse.

Money Earned by Your Children

Another "specifically included" item is "amounts received for the services of a child." When you have a child who is an actor, a musical prodigy, or a streetwalker, and you collect the cash, whose income is it? Well, according to the Code, it's his income, specifically. Of course it's his income; he earned it, didn't he? Why even have such a provision? The answer is that, in some states, parents are considered the legal recipients of their children's earnings. (Remember that under the Code you are taxed on income which you have a right to receive.) In those states, the parents of a child star would have to pile the child's income on top of their own income—and pay a higher rate of tax. So Congress enacts a law which, for federal income tax purposes, overrides any state law. (Congress's job is made considerably more difficult by the fact that there are fifty states, all with different laws.) The income is the child's, even if he doesn't see a dollar of it, even if he can't have it. He earned it, therefore he pays taxes on it. Children are not shielded from the taxing power of the United States Government.

Nor are senior citizens. Another item "specifically included" in gross income is "an amount received as an annuity." There are many complicated variations of annuities, and the tax laws relating to them are equally complex. A very simple example of an annuity is money you get from an insurance company in return for having given it money earlier. You and the insurance company make a deal. You say, for example, "I'll give you $1000 each year until I am sixty-five (say, in ten years). Then, when I turn sixty-five, you give me $1300 each year for as long as I live." You like to do this because you'll be sure to have some money when you retire. The insurance company loves to do it. It takes your money and invests it and earns money on it. That way, it can pay you back more than $1000 each year for even more than ten years, and maybe still have something left over. Besides that, it bets that you won't live very long after you turn sixty-five. It studies the odds (the actuary tables), and it bets that you'll drop dead at seventy-two. Then it keeps everything that remains of what you gave it and buys General Motors stock.

Why are the annuity payments you receive when you turn sixty-five "specifically included" in gross income? It's a question of timing. The fact is, most of them are *not* included. When you were buying that annuity contract—paying $1000 each year for ten years—you were buying it with income which had already been taxed. When you turn sixty-five, you start getting that money back. It wouldn't be fair to include it in gross income and tax it again. (Remember, income is taxed only once.) However, not all of the money you get back is the money you paid in. Some of it is the money the insurance company earned for you on what you paid in. Congress wants you to pay a tax on those earnings.

The problem is that all you get is a sum—$1300 per year. Which part is money you put in, and which part is earnings on that money? It would be nice if you could say, "The first $10,000 I get back is a return of the money I put in—a return of my investment. After that, I get the earnings, which I pay a tax on." That way, you might be dead before you got the earnings, and then you wouldn't give a damn. However, Congress knows that people tend to die. Having a tendency to die doesn't excuse you from paying taxes.

"When you start to get paid back," Congress says, "ask the insurance company how much it expects to pay you over your life. Figure out what percent of that amount is money you paid in. The same percent of each annuity payment is a return of your investment. Anything extra that you receive each year is 'specifically included' in gross income. That is what you pay taxes on."

Suppose the insurance company expects to pay you $13,000 over your life and you have paid $10,000 to the company. Each year, 77 percent ($10,000 ÷ $13,000) of your $1300 annuity (or $1000) is a return of your investment. The rest ($300) is earnings and is "specifically included" in gross income.

Your insurance company will usually provide you with the information you need on questions such as these. The annuity provisions of the Code take up six pages, and the IRS uses more than sixty pages to explain them in regulations. This is not an area to tackle on your own. Also, these annuities are not to be confused with "individual retirement accounts," which are tax-sheltering private pension plans, to be examined in Chapter 13.

Breaks for Football Players?

Divorced women, children, senior citizens—none can escape the taxing power of the government. However, football players have tried. One item "specifically" included in gross income is "prizes and awards." Congress specifically included "prizes and awards" in income because in the 1940s some courts ruled that essay-contest prizes and radio-show giveaways were not income, but gifts (gifts, you will soon see, are excluded from income). Congress didn't agree.

Now in the case of a prize or an award, there is seldom any question as to whose income it is or when it is includable. So why did Congress make "prizes or awards" a "specifically included" item? All Congress is saying here is, "Yes (emphatically), prizes and awards are income." "Prizes and awards" should have been listed under section 61, with salary, pensions, annuities, etc. But they are here under "items specifically included," and it is not the only time that the Code's structure is not entirely consistent.

When Congress included prizes and awards in income, it decided to make one exception—for awards for "genuinely meritorious achievements" which you didn't try specifically to win. Prizes and awards made primarily for "religious, charitable, scientific, educational, artistic, literary, or civic achievement" are not included in income. This exception applies only if you didn't enter yourself in the competition, and only if you made no commitments to render substantial services in the future as a condition of receiving your award.

After all, if you make a conscious effort to win the award, or if you agree to work upon receiving it, it looks more like compensation for services. The Nobel and Pulitzer Prizes are the best-known examples of tax-free awards. Another example is when your town gives you a gold watch just because you are such a wonderful person—that is a prize or award not included in gross income.

Several years ago *Sport* magazine voted Paul Hornung of the Green Bay Packers the Most Valuable Player of the National Football League championship game. Hornung won a shiny new Corvette with a value in excess of $3000. Income? You betcha, said the IRS. Not so, said Hornung. It's a prize or award in recognition of meritorious achievement. I didn't enter the contest—my team entered me. And I don't have to do anything in the future for getting the award. Why is it a meritorious achievement? Because football is "educational." After all, it's a part of the physical education curriculum in nearly every college in the country. Also, being a star football player requires a certain degree of "artistry." Moreover, the skills of a football player are based upon techniques which encompass certain "scientific" principles—you have to be a mathematician to understand the plays. Finally, the President of the United States gave me special leave from the Army to play in the championship game—clearly raising the contest to the level of a "civic" event.

If I'd been his lawyer, I would have argued that the enthusiasm of the fans made the whole thing look like a "religious" experience.

The Tax Court agreed with the IRS.

Not only is Hornung's Corvette "specifically" included in gross income, so is the cash value of all the prizes you win on "The Price Is Right," and the money you win on "Name That Tune." If you plan to enter a TV contest, pick one that pays cash-on-the-barrel. Otherwise, you may have to sell the prizes to pay the taxes.

Taxing Your Political Contributions

There is another item which is "specifically included" in gross income, and here it is a question again of whose income it is. "Transfer of Appreciated Property to Political Organizations," or non-cash political contributions.

If you give stock certificates—or paintings—to the Democratic National Committee, which have increased in value over their "adjusted basis" (which is usually their cost), the difference is "specifically included" in your gross income. It's as though you sold the property to the Committee at a profit, even though you didn't get anything for it—at least directly. (It may be capital income—capital gain—rather than ordinary income, if you held it for more than twelve months, something we'll talk about later.) Why is that income at all? You don't get anything liquid for it or even anything you might liquidate. You don't even get the cash you'll need to pay the tax on the profit. The reason your contribution nonetheless results in income to you is that Congress was afraid that it might otherwise produce income for the political organization.

Contributions to political organizations used to be considered gifts. Contributors to political organizations liked it that way. If they had some stock which they'd bought for $1000 and was now worth $3000, they could make a political contribution of $3000 at a cost of $1000. More important, they could unload a piece of property which had increased in value without paying any income tax on the gain. Had they sold the stock and contributed $3000 in cash, they would have incurred an income tax liability on the $2000 profit. But if they contributed the stock itself, they had no gain, they had no profit, and they paid no tax. (They may have incurred a gift tax liability if the contribution was substantial, but even the gift tax—which is less than the income tax—could be avoided with careful planning.) Contributors were pleased; they could make hefty contributions at a cost of a fraction of the value and pay no tax. Politicians, of course, were very pleased.

This neat little loophole couldn't last forever. Along came the Internal Revenue Service. If the contributor doesn't pay a tax on the increase in value of the stock, the IRS said, then the political organization must pay the tax when the stock is sold. Under the gift tax laws, the "cost" of the stock to the organization is the price at which it was purchased originally by the contributor. If the organization sells it at the increased value, it has a profit which it must pay tax on.

Count on the IRS to spoil a good thing. The position it took posed a serious problem for political groups, who obviously would sell the stock as soon as they got their hands on it. You couldn't pay for campaign buttons with stock certificates. Nor could you pay for campaign buttons with money that went to the federal treasury.

Congress's reaction was swift and decisive, so fast that the IRS couldn't even implement its ruling. This coddling of political contributors could go just so far, Congress said. The result was "Transfer of Appreciated Property to Political Organizations." The contributor pays the tax. It's as though he sold the stock to the political organization and received fair market value in cash. This "deemed profit" is his gain and the gain is "specifically included" in his gross income. The "cost" to the organization is then the value of the stock when it gets it—as though it had paid that price in cash. If it sells it immediately: no profit, no tax. The only reason Congress could drum up for this change was "appropriateness." The Senate Finance Committee wrote: "The Committee believes that it is appropriate to tax the contributor on unrealized appreciation on property transferred to political organizations." Even goodies for taxpayers who make gifts to politicians have their limits.

Life Insurance Premiums

Another item "specifically included" in gross income is the amount of premiums which your employer may pay to purchase term life insurance contracts covering you and other employees. Employers have often provided term life insurance to groups of employees as a fringe benefit of employment, and in the 1950s questions arose as to whether the proportionate cost of providing this insurance should be included in the income of each covered employee. An employee had no right to the premium itself because that went directly to the insurance company. Also, since there is no cash value in term insurance, the policy had no value to the employee while he was alive. And if he died, the benefits didn't go to him anyway.

Some tax specialists convinced the IRS that employer-paid premiums for term insurance (as opposed to whole life insurance with a cash value) should not be includable in the employee's income because he had no right to anything of value. But they didn't convince the Congress. Premiums for group-term life insurance were "specifically included" in the gross income of each covered employee. In Congress's view, the employee received a "substantial economic benefit" from the insurance protection and was relieved of "substantial costs of providing his own insurance protection for his family."

Now you may be thinking, My employer is buying me a group-term life insurance contract of $50,000 and I don't include the premiums he pays in my income. You are correct, because Congress wrote an exception to the general rule of includability. The amount of employer-paid premiums for the first $50,000 of term insurance for employee groups is not treated as income to covered employees.

Why is the premium for the first $50,000 not income? How is it any different from the next $50,000?

It isn't any different. Congress just decided that "from the standpoint of the economy as a whole . . . it is desirable to encourage employers to provide life insurance for their employees." It helps, Congress said, "to keep together family units where the principal breadwinner dies prematurely." There was no logic in the law for excluding the premium for the first $50,000. There was just a policy decision (and probably some heavy lobbying by the insurance industry).

It is because of things like group-term insurance that the tax laws are heavily criticized. Congress sets down rules— such as "everything is income"—and then it makes exceptions, like group-term life insurance premiums. Liberals argue that the tax laws contain too many loopholes for the rich and should be more rigid. Conservatives say that society is complex and we need flexible tax laws which encourage desirable activities. As for group-term insurance, well, it is not a loophole just for the rich because the premiums are usually tax-free to the covered employees only if the insurance is provided to a *group* of employees in *all* income brackets. And yet people not covered by these insurance plans must go out and buy their own insurance with dollars which were included in income—after-tax dollars. You may have ideas of your own on questions such as these. But we are just getting started. Before passing judgment, read on and consider some of the other exceptions in the tax laws which may provide "loopholes" or "flexibility," depending upon your point of view.

These are the more popular items "specifically included" in income; they are the parts of the tax law which tell you when to include income in income, or whether the income belongs to someone else, or that, yes, a particular item is in fact income, but with certain exceptions. Of course there are many more items "specifically included" in gross income. There are some esoteric items which seem to affect about seven people each year. Like "income from mortgages made by joint-stock land banks," or "amounts received as loans from the Commodity Credit Corporation." Also, "the amount of any increase in the suspense account required by paragraph (4) (B) (ii) of section 166(g) (relating to certain debt obligations guaranteed by dealers)." Right. Anything you say. These provisions, and others like them, are clearly aimed at special people with special problems.

As for the items we have discussed, there is nothing magical or sophisticated about them. There is no reason to be confused. Once Congress decided to include in income everything that you have a right to, it had to go one step further and decide whether and when you had a right to it.

FOUR
What Is "Specifically Excluded" from Gross Income?

The best way to avoid paying income taxes on money you get is to be the beneficiary of a life insurance policy of someone who dies, get run over by a truck, get sick, be in a war zone, or buy state and local bonds. Amounts received under these circumstances, among others, are usually "specifically excluded" from gross income. These are the amounts which are not included in gross income even though "everything" is included. These items and others are described in sections 101–124 of the Code, which come after Congress tells you what is included in gross income and what is "specifically included" in gross income on top of all the other things that are included in gross income. Congress does not mention these items too early: You have to go about one hundred pages into the Code before you start to find out what is not included in gross income. You even learn how to use tax credits to reduce the taxes on your income before you learn what is not income.

Remember that section 61 begins, "Except as other-

wise provided . . ." We now come to that "otherwise provided" category—items "specifically *excluded*" from gross
income. These items don't reduce income—only deductions
reduce income. These items never get into gross income in
the first place. They are excluded. Even though "everything" is included in gross income, these items are not.

Why are some items of income excluded from gross income? It's not because they are not income, nor is it so that
rich people won't have to pay taxes. You will see that most
of these items cross the lives of all kinds of people, and that
exclusions from income are not tax loopholes. Congress simply decided, as with the Pulitzer Prize or the premiums for
$50,000 of term insurance, that certain things of value
which you receive should not be taxable. We will examine
these things and why they are not taxed. They are not unlim-
ited in number; you can't hire a tax expert and expect him
to discover a new item of excludable income. There are
certain exclusions—listed and described in the Code. If an
item isn't listed as *specifically* excluded, then it's included.
It's as simple as that—most of the time.

Life Insurance Proceeds

Certain death benefits are not included in gross income.
If somebody dies owning an insurance contract which
names you as the beneficiary, the money you get from the
insurance company is "specifically excluded" from gross income. It doesn't count. As far as the U.S. Government is
concerned, you never get it.

Why? Usually people get life insurance proceeds because
someone close to them dies—a father, a husband—someone
who was supporting them. The proceeds are viewed as indemnity to the beneficiary for the loss of support. They are
as much "reimbursement" as they are "income." The government thinks it would be inappropriate to step in and tax
these proceeds away. Indeed, the tax could be very high; if

the life insurance proceeds were just $50,000, the recipient could be in the 50 percent bracket without a penny of income from other sources. When you buy a life insurance policy to provide for your spouse and children after you die, you don't plan on giving half of it to the federal treasury. And so Congress excludes it from gross income. Would you vote for any congressman who didn't? (Note that the value of an insurance policy is included in the owner's estate, and the estate may have to pay an estate tax.)

If you pay for an insurance policy naming yourself as beneficiary, on the life of someone who dies, the proceeds are still excluded from your gross income. So if you buy an insurance policy on your spouse's life, and name yourself as beneficiary, the proceeds are still excluded from your income. You could even buy an insurance policy on the life of a complete stranger and collect the proceeds tax-free, if you could get him to submit to a physical examination.

Congress does not carry this tax benefit too far. If you buy an outstanding policy *from* someone which insures his life or a third party's life—well, that is too much like an investment—and the proceeds are excludable only up to your cost for the contract. (There is an exception to this rule for business partners who sell contracts on their own lives to one another.)

If you receive a death benefit from your spouse's employer, only the first $5000 is excludable from gross income. The rest is included and taxed. Why does it matter whether your deceased spouse bought a life insurance policy or whether his employer pays you an amount of money at his death (something which your spouse might have bargained for)? Is it any more appropriate to tax it away if the boss delivers it than if the insurance company does? Of course not. But if you give a taxpayer a dime you know he'll want Fort Knox. Employees all over the country would be making private arrangements with their employers: "Don't pay me $25,000 next year or the year after; pay me $22,000 each

year and pay the difference to my family only when I die."
He wouldn't pay an income tax on the $3000 next year, or
the year after, and his wife wouldn't pay an income tax on
the accumulated fund when she gets it. Over twenty or
thirty years you could shelter a considerable amount of income. And then who would pay for the Cruise Missile? Congress gives the widow $5000 to cover funeral, floral, and
legal expenses. The rest is included in gross income.

Unlike alimony, those life insurance proceeds are excluded from gross income whether they are paid immediately in a lump sum or in installments over a period of time
(but any interest earned on the unpaid portion over the
extended time is considered income when paid). This nod to
periodic payments came about when the Congress of 1939
noted, "There are vultures and professional racketeers who
prey upon the widows and orphans where benefits from
insurance policies are paid to them in a lump sum." In the
formation of tax legislation, widows and orphans may not do
too well, but they always fare better than professional racketeers. They also fare better than confidence men, swin-
dlers, and "racketeering groups of gougers." "Racketeering
groups of gougers," in particular, get no sympathy from
Congress.

Sue 'Em

If you can't arrange for the death of someone insured
under a life insurance policy which names you as the beneficiary, try getting run over by a truck. Break six bones, have
four operations, spend nine weeks in the hospital (all of this
is covered by medical insurance); have your salary cut off,
suffer extreme pain, humiliation, and inconvenience; be un-
able to have a "fulfilling marital relationship" with your
spouse; and lose partial motion in your middle toe. Settle
with the truck driver's insurance company for $539,000.
Damages received on account of personal injuries are "spe-

cifically excluded" from gross income. No tax. You never got it—$539,000 of excluded income. That could be the equivalent of as much as $1,700,000 of included income, because the government might take nearly 70 percent of the included income. How long would you have to work, how many laws would you have to break, to make $1,700,000?

Why isn't this money included in income? For the same reason as the life insurance proceeds: It is indemnity, this time for your pain, suffering, and losses. If you get paid back for being mauled by a truck, should you turn over half the money to the government? Did your congressman get run over by the truck?

The money you get from your health insurance company to pay for your medical bills is also "specifically excluded" from gross income. Regardless of whether you or your employer paid for the health insurance contract, the proceeds are not considered income to you so long as they are reimbursement for, or payment of, medical expenses. *Excess* reimbursements from a policy which your employer paid for are income, but not from a policy which you paid for yourself. If you receive medical expense reimbursements both from your insurance company and from the truck driver's company in the form of damages, it's all excluded. However, if you claimed a deduction for medical expenses and are later reimbursed, the reimbursement is income up to the amount of the deduction you claimed, regardless of the source of the reimbursement. You cannot receive money tax-free when it reimburses an expense for which you already claimed a deduction.

What about the premiums for medical insurance which your employer paid for you? You know that these are not included in income either. If Congress wanted employers to provide term life insurance, obviously it wanted them to provide medical insurance too.

From a tax standpoint, suffering a disaster is not all that bad—but you must be careful here because the tax benefits depend upon the kind of disaster you suffer. The damage award which you receive from the truck driver's insurance company is excluded from income (except for reimbursements for medical expenses which you deducted), even though it may be based in part on the amount of salary you lost because of your injuries. Those lost earnings which would have been taxable if you received them for working are tax-free when you receive them because you couldn't work.

On the other hand, if you suffer a loss of wages because of an accident which is your own fault or because you become ill, payments which you receive from a disability insurance contract are not always accorded such favorable treatment. Disability pay from an insurance contract you purchased yourself, or from a fund you contributed to, are excluded from gross income. But if your employer paid for the contract (and the premiums were not income to you), then the general rule is that payments under the contract are includable in income, and taxable. With disability insurance, you cannot get both tax-free coverage and tax-free proceeds. (There are exceptions if your injuries are extremely severe.) So if you are going to be laid up for a while without pay, and if you don't have your own disability insurance contract, from a tax standpoint you are better off if it is the fault of someone you can sue.

You would think that all amounts received as compensation for lost wages would be treated the same way, either all taxable or all tax-free. What difference does it make whether you are compensated by the truck driver's liability insurance contract or by your employer's disability insurance contract? (To add to the complexity, workman's compensation benefits are not included in income.) Distinctions like these permeate the tax laws. Sometimes the legislative history provides a clear and rational explanation for the differences. Sometimes that history is hopelessly obscure (which happens to be the case here) or totally confused, and then tax theorists have plenty to argue about. These laws develop over time—different periods, different problems, different thinking. Some people say that the Congress should sort all this out so that the average taxpayer can keep it straight. Maybe it should. The problem is that it might take longer to sort it out than it took to mess it up in the first place, and then we would be right back where we started. So for now let's keep going and do the best we can.

Bullets and Bonds

There is a simpler way to exclude your salary from gross income: Be an enlisted man in a combat zone. His salary is specifically excluded from gross income. (For officers, only the first $500 per month is excluded.) Soldiers of fortune beware: You cannot fight for the Israelis or the Angolans while you are waiting for the next U.S. war. You must be an enlisted man or an officer in the Armed Forces of the United States.

This apparent chauvinism on Capitol Hill is carried just so far. One item of income which seems like a natural for specific exclusion is interest paid by agencies of the U.S. Government. When you buy a Treasury bill, for example, you are lending money to the U.S. Government—the Treasury bill is an I.O.U.—and the government pays you interest. Or if you buy a Federal National Mortgage Association (Fannie Mae) bond, or a Federal Home Loan Bank Board bond, you are lending your money to a government agency and it pays you interest. In all these loans the interest is nothing extraordinary—usually two or three points below prime. Does the government then turn around and tax away a part of the measly interest it pays? After you're patriotic enough to loan money to your government at such lousy interest rates? You bet it does. After all, the money the government pays you is no different from anybody else's money. It's green, it's good, you can spend it, save it, burn it, lose it. Why shouldn't you be taxed on it? The interest rate may be nothing fantastic, but then your risk is almost zero. After General Motors, AT&T, and New York City are long gone, the U.S. Government will still be there paying its lousy interest. Only the Church will outlast the U.S. Government, and it doesn't sell bonds.

Curiously, the U.S. Government does not tax interest which states and local governments pay to people who loan money to *them.* Only to itself. Interest paid by state or local governments on their debts is "specifically excluded" from gross income. It's not that the Congress has such high regard for the states. Two hundred years ago, the framers of the Constitution—most of whom were states-righters—got a jump on the Congress and prohibited federal taxation of interest on state or local obligations. In fact, Congress tried to tax that kind of income once, and the Supreme Court vetoed it.

Interest on state and local obligations is the "tax-sheltered" or "tax-free" income you always hear about. You may see advertisements in the *Wall Street Journal* or the *New York Times* that read: "In the opinion of Bond Counsel, interest on the Bonds is exempt under existing statutes and court decisions from Federal income taxes." They are describing state and local government bonds.

Your state wants to build a superhighway; your town needs a new hospital. How do they pay for these things? They borrow money from you; they give you an I.O.U., i.e., a bond. They pay you interest on what they borrow, usually less than your savings bank pays, but you don't care because that money is all yours. You don't have to pay any taxes on that interest. It's specifically excluded from gross income. It's tax-free.

Example: You lend your town $10,000—you buy a $10,-000 bond—and it pays you interest at 5 percent, or $500 per year. Terrible interest. But you pay no tax on that $500. You can spend every penny of it. If you are in the 50 percent tax bracket, to have $500 after taxes you would have to earn $1000. That would require a 10 percent return on your $10,000 investment. Your savings bank cannot pay you 10 percent. Your town, by paying you 5 percent interest tax-free is providing you with as much spendable income as you would get from 10 percent taxable interest elsewhere. (Remember these figures are for the 50 percent bracket.) All this is part of the larger subject of tax shelters. We'll return to tax-sheltered income in Chapter 13. You'll see that tax shelters are not everything they are rumored to be.

Priests and Presents

If you prefer not to get caught up in the complexities of tax-sheltered state or local bonds, but are still desirous of having some tax-free income, you might become a priest. You will recall that, as company president living rent-free in the company suite, the rental value of the apartment is income to you. But if you're a "minister of the gospel," and your church gives you a place to live, the value of that place is "specifically excluded" from gross income. Even if it gives you the money to rent your own place, the money is "specifically excluded" from gross income. Compared to racketeering groups of gougers, clergymen fare very well on Capitol Hill. In case you are wondering, the IRS has ruled that rabbis are "ministers of the gospel" as well.

Another way to have tax-free income is to be the recipient of a gift. Amounts received as a gift are "specifically excluded" from gross income. The same is true for inheritances. If someone gives you $5000, you don't have to pay tax on that. It's a gift. (He may have to pay a gift tax, however, which is a whole other can of worms. If he doesn't pay the gift tax, then you will have to pay it—still more worms.)

One reason people who receive gifts aren't taxed is that they probably wouldn't report it anyway. Why pass a law you can't enforce?

Another reason is simple practicality. The great majority of gifts are made between parents and children. Do you want your children to pay tax on their Christmas presents?

A third reason is that people who receive gifts tend not to have much other income and don't have to pay taxes anyway, or pay tax at a very low rate. There's no money in taxing them. The people who give gifts, on the other hand —this is where the money is. Slap the tax on the pocketbook, not on the outstretched palm. Tax the guy who's got so much money he's giving it away. Congressmen are sly foxes. (If you're one of those passing around large gifts, don't figure the tax consequences with a do-it-yourself kit. Not only the gift but also your estate is involved.)

Another reason that people aren't taxed on gifts they receive is that what they receive has already been taxed once. The donor paid a tax when he made the money he gives away, so those dollars have already been clobbered by the Internal Revenue laws, and the donor is merely sharing the consumption power that remains. In fact, for gifts of *income* on property (instead of gifts of property), there is an exception to the rule that gifts are tax-free to the recipient. If somebody gives you a gift of a $5000 savings account or stock worth $5000, you are not liable for income tax on that $5000. If he keeps the account or the stock, but gives you all rights in the interest or dividends before they have been earned, those interest or dividend payments are included in your gross income. Why? Because when those earnings come directly to you no one has paid tax on them. Gifts are tax-free only if the property given has already been taxed.

You will recall that if you owe somebody money and he says, "Forget about it," that is income to you. Why isn't that a gift? If you could get him to write, "Out of the kindness of my heart, and in grateful recognition of your magnificence as a human being, forget about it," then you'd be thinking like a lawyer and you might turn taxable debt-forgiveness into a tax-free gift. Would he write that down for you? It would depend on whether, after forgiving your debt, he wanted to pay a gift tax too. Also, you might be tripped up by a principle in the tax law which the IRS uses in scrutinizing all transactions. It is the principle of "Substance Over Form." Look at what is really happening, not at what somebody calls it. Even if your creditor wrote down what you asked him to, the IRS might disregard it.

Meals and Lodging

What else can be "specifically excluded" from gross income? Consider the recurring and tantalizing item called "Meals and Lodging Furnished for the Convenience of the Employer." (Not to be confused with the business lunch deduction, which we'll get to in Chapter 5.) You may remember that the rental value of the company suite which you live in as president is income to you. Well, that rule does not apply if the suite is on the company's premises, and if it is to the company's advantage to have you live there, and if in fact you must live there as a condition of your employment. Under these circumstances, the value of the suite is "specifically excluded" from gross income. Note that your living there must be a substantive condition of employment. You can't merely have the Board of Directors say, "If you want to be president here you have to live in the company suite." It must be necessary for you to live there in order to do your job. For example, the President of the United States must live in the White House, therefore the rental value of the White House is not income to him.

This rule applies to all employees, not just to presidents. Managers of hotels often have to live in the hotel, and then the rental value of their hotel apartment is specifically excluded from gross income. But no arrangement is a sure thing in this area of tax law. As an example, the president of a hotel in New Orleans lived in an apartment in the hotel and claimed that the rental value was excludable from gross income. Not so, said the court. Her husband had preceded her as hotel president, and they had lived in a house far away from the hotel. It was after her husband died that she moved into the hotel. So where was the proof that living in the hotel was essential to her job as president?

The same basic rules apply to meals. If meals are furnished to you by your employer on his premises, and if it is to his advantage to have you take your meals there, the value of the meals is specifically excluded from gross income. (It is not necessary that you be required to dine there, but only that your employer considers it important that you do.) One company rented a suite in a nearby hotel for daily luncheon conferences. Officers were expected to attend in order to get together and talk all at once rather than through separate conferences which took too much time. That was a sufficient employer advantage for the tax court. Was the hotel on the premises? Not technically, but since the suite was rented every day, it was as good as being the employer's premises.

Congress specifically excluded the value of certain meals and lodging to avoid continuous squabbles between taxpayers and the IRS. Prior to 1954, the IRS would try to tax the value of all meals and lodging. Taxpayers would argue: "I'm required to eat and sleep there. It's not a benefit. I don't even like it." And the IRS would say, "But you get less salary because you are provided with room and board." And then they would settle down to bickering over whether the taxpayer could get more salary if he lived off the premises. In 1954 Congress stepped in and said, If you must live on the premises, or are encouraged to dine there, then it is not income.

Did that stop the bickering? Not at all. State troopers fought for years with the IRS over the the includability of the value of meals. State troopers sometimes get meal allowances because they are required to eat in restaurants near the highways they patrol, and may be called away from a meal at any time and have to buy another one later on. Income? It all depended on which part of the country they lived in. One state trooper in Minnesota argued that since the state was his employer, all the highways were the "premises" of his employer. Since he was required to eat at restaurants on the highway, the meals were "furnished for the employer's convenience on his premises." And he won.

Another state trooper, living in New Hampshire, fared worse. There the court said it didn't buy this "metaphysical concept" that all of the state's territory is the "premises" of the employer. Also, the court said, the meals must be furnished "in kind" (food, not cash).

Same facts. Two state troopers. Two states. Different results. Hardly a uniform application of the law. Often in the tax law two taxpayers in the same situation get treated differently by different courts. That simply happens under the American judicial system. One taxpayer lives in one part of the country, and the court there agrees with him. Another taxpayer somewhere else lands in a court that agrees with the IRS. There is no point in trying to reconcile the different results. Different judges interpret the laws differently. The laws were written by lawyers who suspected that they might be interpreted differently. I know of lawyers who in one year have persuaded people at the National Office of the IRS that a law should be interpreted in a certain way, and then in the next year persuaded other people at the National Office that it should be interpreted in exactly the opposite way. It's not surprising that two judges thousands of miles apart can give different interpretations. If the law being interpreted is an important one and the various courts continue to disagree, the Supreme Court takes a case and decides what the law means once and for all. Of course, Supreme Court decisions are also subject to interpretation, and sometimes the lower courts just go back to disagreeing over what the Supreme Court decision means.

The Supreme Court finally decided a case involving a

state trooper's meal allowance. It held that the allowance was in fact income to the trooper. The Court said that, apart from the question of his employer's needs, the trooper received cash, not food, while the law required that food be furnished. The Supreme Court didn't resolve the question of whether the highway was the state's premises. (It didn't have to resolve that question because the trooper had already lost the case on the distinction between cash and food.) Now suppose Minnesota adopts a system under which its troopers can stop at certain designated restaurants on the highways and *sign* for the meals, with the bills sent to the state. No cash. Just food. Then what? It would seem that the value of the meals would not be income—*if* the highway (and the restaurant on it) were considered the state's premises. So then that would have to be resolved. And on it goes.

Scholarships

There is another popular kind of income which is "specifically excluded" from gross income. Amounts received as "scholarships from educational organizations," or "fellowship grants." The tax law defines these terms to include not only tuition, but also amounts received for room and board, laundry, and similar accommodations and services (or the value of these items). The terms also include amounts received as a family allowance. And it is all tax-free.

Those of you who have received a scholarship or a grant know that in fact it is not that simple. The rules in this area get pretty complex. Here's why. When it passed this law Congress was worried that it might be creating an income-tax-free society in our educational institutions. As long as scholarships and grants are not considered items of income, the universities bestowing them are not required to pay payroll taxes on them (social security, unemployment, etc.). There would be no income tax, and no payroll tax. It was all very easy. Congress was afraid that before long professors would be getting "fellowship grants" instead of salaries. So it threw in a catch: In order to be tax-free, the money has to be applied toward study or research intended primarily to "further the education or training of the recipient." It cannot be used primarily to pay for teaching or research services for the benefit of the university.

Now it often occurs that someone receives a scholarship or a grant primarily for his own "education and training" but is nonetheless required to teach or conduct research for the university on a part-time basis. So Congress threw in another catch. When the recipient provides teaching or research services, an appropriate portion of the grant must be treated as compensation for those services and included in income. This particular catch presented a problem to students in pursuit of a degree who had to teach or do research as part of the degree program. So Congress said that this catch was not applicable to them, and the entire scholarship was excludable from income.

Congress was mostly concerned about students who were not pursuing a degree. What were they doing if not working toward a degree? Were they furthering their education or just working for the university? These "students" must always allocate the amount of the grant between "education and training" and teaching or research. And for these people there is still another catch. Lest someone try to allocate $50 to teaching (included in income) and $2000 to education and training (excluded from income), Congress said that for students not pursuing a degree, the most money they can allocate to education and training is $300 per month. Anything over that is income to them. And they are entitled to such an exclusion for only thirty-six months, consecutive or otherwise. Amounts in excess of $300 monthly, or received for more than thirty-six months, will always be treated as taxable compensation for services, whatever allocation is attempted. In effect Congress is saying that when a student who is not pursuing a degree receives money in excess of

$300 monthly for tuition, meals, lodging, and a family allowance, the excess must be viewed as compensation for services.

What happens if you receive the entire grant during the first month? When that happens, you can pretend you received it evenly over the period of your studies—subject to the thirty-six-month limitation. If you couldn't do that, you would use up your exclusion in the first month.

The law on scholarships and fellowship grants is heavily litigated. The intelligentsia of this country does not just roll over and pay taxes on command. It's in there scrapping with the IRS along with the nation's biggest industries. It has always been that way. Congress wrote all these rules in the first place because the university people and the IRS were constantly fighting over whether a grant or a fellowship was a gift (tax-free) or compensation for services. Congress thought it was establishing "clear-cut" guidelines for determining when scholarships and fellowship grants were excluded from gross income. So clear-cut were Congress's guidelines that since 1954, when the guidelines were set down, the IRS has issued more than 130 rulings on individual cases and has gone to court not less than 150 times.

The area is heavily litigated because the tax status of a grant is still always a question of fact. For example, if a university offers a recent physics graduate a fellowship grant on the condition that his research pertain to the nuclear development contract that the university has with the government, it looks more like compensation for services. On the other hand, if he can do research in any area he chooses ("but we are equipped for research in only two areas, the nuclear project and the project on the velocity of snails"), that looks more like a real grant, though the IRS may not be convinced.

There are only two clear cases. If you're just out of high school and you get a four-year scholarship to study at the university and otherwise partake of its facilities, that is a tax-free scholarship. If you're a Nobel Prize-winning microbiologist, and the university invites you to come and conduct your research there and, while you are there, teach three classes a week, all for a "grant" of $42,000 annually, that isn't a scholarship or fellowship grant. Anything in between will be scrutinized by the IRS.

Little wonder. The way that Americans try to take advantage of the Internal Revenue laws is shameful. In the late 1960s, the winner of a national beauty pageant got a four-year scholarship to the educational institution of her choice. Tax-free? She also had to model, make personal appearances for the company that sponsored the pageant, and do other kinds of promotion. The IRS said there were too many conditions attached, so the scholarship wasn't primarily for her benefit. (She also tried to treat the scholarship as a nontaxable prize or an award. Remember "prizes and awards" for literary, artistic, or civic achievements where you didn't enter the competition? It didn't work, did it?)

Soon after that, a high school baseball player signed on with a major-league club. He agreed to play for the club's minor-league team. The club agreed to pay him for that. This was obviously an employment contract—compensation for services. The club also agreed to "give" him a "scholarship" under its "scholarship plan" so that he could attend a nearby college. Was the scholarship included in gross income? Of course it was.

There was also a high school language teacher who took a leave of absence from her school to study at the Sorbonne. She was paid her full salary and even given expenses, all of which she claimed was a scholarship. Unfortunately, the school had sent her to the Sorbonne to prepare herself to teach a new course, a course which the school had to offer in order to qualify for federal funds. It had sent her with the understanding that she would return to the school and teach the course. The IRS disagreed with her claim that she had received a scholarship. So did the Tax Court.

On and on it goes. Teachers, students, and researchers, like most people, just hate to pay those taxes. Scores of them slug it out with the IRS every year. Some day the rules may become more stable, if Congress doesn't set down any more "clear-cut" guidelines.

As you can see, it is not easy to accumulate income that is "specifically excluded" from gross income. Running under trucks is no way to make a living, tax-free insurance proceeds are small compensation for the death of a close family member, and the tax benefits of a meal allowance probably would not have justified moving to Minnesota to become a state trooper. Still, there is something in the Internal Revenue Code for everyone. If you own stock in almost any domestic corporation, and if the stock pays dividends, the first $100 of dividends that you receive each year is "specifically excluded" from gross income. That line on the front of your 1040 form—"Dividends _____ Less Exclusion _____" —is there because of the $100 specific exclusion for dividends. Congress wants you to invest in the stock market, and practically any stockholding taxpayer can benefit from the provision. No strings attached. The dividend doesn't have to be furnished on the premises of your employer, the money you paid for the stock doesn't have to be used to build a hospital, and it doesn't matter whether the dividend is salary to you (if you are a full-time investor) or a kind of compensation for pain and suffering (if you have as much success in the stock market as I do). As long as it's a dividend, it's tax-free up to $100. The government is not being as generous as you might think. Those dividends you receive come from the corporation's earnings, and Congress has already taxed those earnings anyway.

The Code lists many more items "specifically excluded" from gross income—some more relevant than others for individual taxpayers. Some of these are very simple: living expenses paid under a homeowner's policy if your house is damaged and you must live elsewhere while it is repaired; or mustering-out payments received from the Armed Forces. Social Security benefits are excluded from income under the Social Security laws.

Other items: "Income taxes paid by lessee corporations," "improvements by lessee on lessor's property," and "income from discharge of indebtedness on certain business property." Do you really care? You know about them anyway if you are that much involved in business. There is also an exclusion for income received for certain "sports programs conducted for the American Red Cross." If you plan to conduct a sports program for the American Red Cross, see your tax advisor.

That is gross income. After you have added up everything that is included, and then added to that all the things that are "specifically included," and left out all the things that are "specifically excluded," you have gross income.

Does it seem kind of complicated? All that just to add up your income? In fact, it's the simplest part of the Code. From here on, things only get worse.

Should it be so complicated? You have seen that there are usually reasons for each rule and for each exception to the rule. Do the reasons justify the complexity? Would it be better just to include everything in income, with no exceptions, and lower the tax rates? If you have never been run over by a truck, received life insurance proceeds, or gotten a scholarship, you may feel that there should be no exceptions. Unfortunately for you, there are lots of people who have received insurance benefits or scholarships, and they write to their congressmen too. So here we are.

Knowing what your gross income is does not tell you what your tax is or even how to compute it. All it tells you is what the total of your income is for tax purposes. Congress does not impose a tax on the total of your income. It taxes only a part of your income. It makes you compute your gross income so that it can look at what you've got while, licking its chops, it decides which part of it to tax. Once it knows how much you've got, it always lets you reduce that by a certain amount and then it imposes a tax on what is left over.

You get to reduce your gross income in two stages. First you reduce it by certain amounts to arrive at what Congress calls your "adjusted gross income." Then you reduce it again by certain other amounts to arrive at what Congress calls your "taxable income." It is on your taxable income that Congress imposes a tax—from 14 to 70 percent.

FIVE
Reducing Your Income to Adjusted Gross Income

"Adjusted gross income" is "gross income" as adjusted.

What is it adjusted by? It is adjusted by whatever the Code says it is adjusted by. More important, it is adjusted down. It is never adjusted up. How could it be adjusted up if everything is already included?

Adjusted gross income is merely gross income reduced by certain deductions. Deductions are amounts of money (with certain exceptions) which you spend (with certain exceptions) which the Congress says can be applied to reduce your gross income. Deductions should not be confused with tax credits. Deductions reduce income on which tax is to be computed, while tax credits reduce the tax itself. Some people think that if they have a $100 deduction, they reduce their taxes by $100. Not so. Only tax credits perform magic like that. Deductions should also not be confused with "items specifically excluded from gross income." Items specifically excluded from gross income are amounts of money you *receive* which Congress says you can pretend you didn't receive. Deductions are amounts that you *spend*.

Why can you reduce your income by certain amounts that you spend? Reasons will be supplied as the various deductible items are described. However, you can be certain that there is one of two reasons. First, there is a policy justifying the deduction—a decision by Congress that certain expenditures should be encouraged. If you don't buy the policy justification, then you can assume that the whole thing is a boondoggle fashioned by hungry congressmen seeking the favors of rich constituents.

The Code allows many deductions. Some of them can be used to reduce gross income to *adjusted* gross income, which is what we are talking about now. These deductions are more business than personal in nature. Most of them represent amounts spent in order to make money.

Other deductions are used to reduce that *now-adjusted* gross income to *taxable* income. These deductions are often more personal in nature, representing amounts spent to live, and a group of them are popularly called "itemized deductions." An alternative to these personal "itemized deductions" is to take advantage of the "zero bracket amount," which used to be called the "standard deduction." We'll talk about these personal deductions in the next chapter. Whatever you do about your personal living deductions does not affect your right to take most business deductions from your gross income to arrive at *adjusted* gross income. Most business deductions are for everybody.

There are many business deductions which may be used to offset gross income. The chief ones are deductions for expenses related to your trade or business—your job or career. These expenses include transportation and traveling expenses, and, in some cases, entertainment and education expenses. Moving expenses may also be deducted from gross income.

Trade or Business Deductions

To understand your "business deductions," consider what happens in an actual business.

Let us say you are in the business of selling pencils whole-sale—lots of pencils. First, you have to pay for the pencils. You also have to pay for your office and your warehouse. Then you have to pay for a lot of other things just to operate —lights, heat, insurance, a telephone, and someone to answer it when someone calls and says, "Hey, we want pencils." All these are necessary expenses just so that you can sell your pencils. Now the government wants its share too. The Congress aims to tax the earnings of an individual at rates as high as 50 percent, and a corporation of any size is taxed at nearly 50 percent. But Congress knows that first it has to let you deduct all those expenses. If it just said, "We don't care about all those expenses—that's your problem— we just know that every time you take in $2 for pencils we want one dollar," clearly you would not be selling pencils very long. It would cost you at least $1 to sell the pencils and the government would take the other dollar. Therefore no one would have any pencils except people who could buy them from someone who bootlegs pencils. Well, Congress does not like to encourage bootlegging. So it accepts the principle that it costs money to make money in a business, and in its wisdom it extends this insight even to people who don't own businesses, but who work for someone else. And that's what we will talk about now: deductions for people who work for someone else. In Chapter 10 we will talk about what happens if you own the business or have property or some other sideline which generates income.

If you don't own a business, but work for someone else, frequently there are times when you find you must spend money in connection with his trade or business. And frequently you submit proof of your expenditures and he reimburses you and that's that. Congress, in its generosity, says that you can deduct *any* expenditures that you make in connection with the owner's trade or business, provided he reimburses you. Which, essentially, adds up to nothing. The one cancels out the other. The reimbursement is income (everything is income) but if the reimbursement exactly matches the expenditure and you have already accounted to your employer, you can just forget about it. On your tax return you don't have to include the reimbursements in income and deduct the expenditures. You don't have to do anything (although the IRS asks you to state on your return that your expenses matched your reimbursements).

Now these business expenses that you made have to be accounted for by someone. And usually your employer requires you to submit proof of the expenditure in a manner which meets certain substantiation requirements of the IRS, and then your employer accounts to the government. It becomes his problem instead of yours. If the expense was not legitimate, the deduction will be disallowed to him. The Service does it this way because when you spend money for your employer and fully account to him, you are just your employer's agent. The expense is really his expense. Also, it is easier to audit one employer than twenty-five (or 2500) employees.

Suppose your employer reimburses you but does *not* make you account to him for your expenses. For example, he just pays you additional salary which is intended to cover the business expenses you are expected to make. If you don't account to your employer, obviously he cannot account to the government, and so it is up to you to justify and substantiate the expense. In that case, you must include the reimbursement in income, and deduct your expenses. You must also be prepared to show that the expenses were made for business purposes (we will return to that problem in a moment).

More to the point: What expenditures made in connection

with your employment can you deduct from gross income if your employer does *not* reimburse you fully or at all? What can you deduct when it is actually coming out of your own pocket? The rule is this: Unless you are an outside salesman, you can deduct from gross income amounts spent for transportation, and you can deduct amounts for traveling—which include transportation, meals, lodging, and other expenses which you incur while "away from home." Only those unreimbursed expenses and *no* others can be deducted from gross income. (Outside salesmen can always deduct all expenses. Also, moving expenses are a special case, as we shall see.) Why only these particular ones? To my knowledge, Congress has never told us. Other expenses which you incur as an employee may be deductible from adjusted gross income as itemized deductions, and we will get to that.

When you deduct unreimbursed transportation or traveling expenses, obviously you must account for them yourself. You must list them on your return (after including any partial reimbursement in income), and be able to substantiate them if you are audited. So let's look at these deductible expenses more closely.

Transportation and Travel

Transportation expenses are amounts spent on buses, taxis, subways, cars, trains, airplanes, even rickshaws or gondolas, while on your employer's business but not actually in a "travel" status. (You will soon see that, for income tax purposes, the term "travel" has a special meaning.) If you deliver a letter across town and pay for the taxi ride yourself, you can deduct that from gross income. If you use your car, the cost of gas and tolls is deductible. Who keeps record of expenses like that? Many people do. For instance, people like teachers, who may have to go to several schools during the day and pay for the gasoline or bus fare themselves.

They keep track of that. If they use their cars regularly, they also keep track of an allocable portion of repairs and other expenses of owning a car. They even "depreciate" a portion of their cars—a matter we will examine in Chapter 10. And they get a nice deduction from gross income at the end of the year even if they use the "zero bracket amount" or standard deduction. Of course, any partial reimbursement is income which offsets the deductible amount.

The only transportation expenses you cannot deduct are commuting expenses. Congress won't subsidize your journey from home to work and back again. Everybody has to go to work. Why should the Government help pay for it? The teacher who goes from school to school cannot deduct transportation expenses between home and work, and vice versa, but only the expenses during work.

IRS regulations contain no special rules for substantiating "transportation" expenses, but common sense tells you to keep receipts of your expenditures whenever possible. If a receipt cannot be obtained, make your own record of the expense soon after it is made. If you use your car partly for your employer's business and partly for personal reasons, it is important to have a sensible method for determining the total number of business miles, so that you can allocate operating and repair costs between business and pleasure.

If you don't keep records for automobile expenses, you can use the IRS's "cost per business mile" figure, which is presently 17 cents per mile for the first 15,000 miles (10 cents for additional miles), but which sometimes changes. Even with this method, you must know how many business miles you drove.

Let me make one point about these business-expense deductions before we go any further. Any business expense—whether incurred as an employee or as a proprietor—is deductible only if it is an "ordinary and necessary" expense. This "ordinary and necessary" rule is the initial requirement for the deductibility of business expenses and has a meaning all its own which we shall look at more closely in Chapter 10. In this chapter we shall assume that the expenses are "ordinary and necessary" and we will concentrate on the other requirements affecting their deductibility by employees.

"Travel" expenses include transportation costs, meals, lodging, telephone calls, laundry, tips, and other amounts that you spend while on the road on business. But if you are an employee, you must be *away from home* to deduct these expenses. When are you "away from home"? You would think that you would know when you are away from home, but just because you are away from home for most purposes doesn't mean that you are away from home for tax purposes.

The problems you encounter with being "away from home" are either not being away long enough, or being away too long. Suppose you work in New York City, fly to Chicago in the morning on business, eat lunch there, spill coffee on your tie and have it dry-cleaned in a one-hour dry cleaner, work all day and return to New York late that afternoon. Assume that your employer reimburses you only for the cost of the plane fare. Can you deduct the cost of the meal and the dry-cleaning? No. You were not "away from home." You might have been 800 miles away from home geographically, but for tax purposes you were not away from home. (If your employer did not reimburse you for your plane fare, you could still deduct that—not as a "travel" expense, but as a "transportation" expense.)

Suppose you work in New York City, drive 90 miles to New Haven, Connecticut, primarily on business, have lunch, get your tie cleaned, work all day, spend the night with your paramour, and then drive back to New York City the next day. Assuming you are reimbursed for gas and tolls, you can now deduct the lunch and the dry-cleaning expenses.

Suppose you work in New York City, fly to Chicago early in the morning, attend a meeting, have lunch, clean your tie, and then, since it has already been a long day and you have another meeting in the afternoon, you rent a hotel room and take a nap. (Maybe you have a paramour in Chicago too.) Then you attend your meeting and fly home late that night. Now you can deduct not only the lunch and the dry-cleaning, but also the cost of the hotel.

The reason for all of this is that, according to the IRS, you are "away from home" only if you are away "overnight," or if your trip is long enough to require you to "sleep or rest" before completing your work. The results of this rule—some of which we have just seen—do not always appear logical, and the IRS might question whether it was "necessary" for you to stay overnight in New Haven or rent a hotel room in Chicago. But assuming that your actions are justifiable, these are the results which flow from the "away from home" test.

Why does the IRS use this "overnight" or "sleep or rest" standard? Because even though you are away from home geographically when you fly to Chicago, have lunch, and return the same day, you would have had lunch even if you didn't fly to Chicago. Why should the lunch be deductible just because you had it in Chicago? A construction worker may drive 70 miles a day every day to get to a job. He's away from home too, but should his lunch be deductible every single day? Congress first enacted the law with the "away from home" language in 1939. If you went practically anywhere over 20 miles back then you were really away from home and you incurred expenses that you wouldn't have incurred if you stayed at home. Jets and superhighways have made the 1939 language obsolete. The IRS now interprets it to mean "overnight" or "sleep or rest," and the Supreme Court has said that that is okay.

This away-from-home rule can hurt the IRS in the case of some taxpayers. If the taxpayer who rests at the Chicago hotel is in a high tax bracket, he might actually save money by staying at the hotel. Suppose during his one-day trip to Chicago he spends $30 on meals and $5 on getting his tie

cleaned. If he doesn't sleep or rest, none of the $35 total is deductible. However, if he spends another $30 for a room at the hotel, the entire $65 in expenses for the day is deductible. As we will see in Chapter 6, if he pays taxes on his top income at the 50 percent rate, the $65 deduction is worth a tax savings to him of $32.50 (for each dollar he reduces his income, he pays 50 cents less in tax). By paying an extra $30 for the hotel, the trip ends up costing him only $32.50 ($65 less the $32.50 tax savings) instead of $35. The government pays for the rest of the trip by letting him reduce his tax liability by $32.50. Sometimes it's nice to be rich even for tax purposes.

Suppose you work on East 52nd Street in New York, go to Brooklyn on business, have lunch there, get your tie cleaned, spend the night with your mistress, and return home the next morning. Clearly you have been away "overnight," but can you deduct the cost of the lunch and the dry-cleaning? Unfortunately for New Yorkers and other denizens of big cities, the entire metropolitan area where you work is considered to be your "home," however much time you spend sleeping around it. Notice also that throughout this discussion we have started your trip from the place where you "work." This is because your "home" for purposes of the travel-expense deduction is your principal place of business, not your residence. So if you live in Westchester County or any suburb of a big city, but work in the city, you don't get a deduction for spending the night in town after a late meeting.

Sometimes you stay away from home too long. If you stay away too long, you may start to get a new home. Once you have a new home, you're not away from home any longer, and then "traveling" expenses are not deductible.

If you live and work in New York but are sent to your company's branch operation in New Haven for a week, obviously you are away from home and all unreimbursed traveling expenses are deductible. Even if you are told to stay an

additional week, you're still away from home. Now suppose the branch manager gets sick, and you are told to stay there until he recovers. For tax purposes you're away from home. Then it begins to look as though he will be sick for some time, so you rent your apartment in New York for the summer, and get an apartment in New Haven. You're starting to get a new home, but you don't have to live in a hotel all summer to keep yourself in a "traveling" status, and so for tax purposes you are still away from home. Finally the branch manager dies, and you are told to stay there until a new branch manager can be found. You rent your New York apartment through Christmas, and find a girl friend in New Haven. You're probably still away from home (although it is becoming a close call). One day you get a phone call: "You're the branch manager until further notice." You rent the New York apartment for a year and move into a bigger apartment in New Haven with your girl friend. Guess what. You've got a new home, and you are not away from it. The IRS says that you are no longer away from home once you settle in a new place and the length of your stay away from home becomes "indefinite."

If you are married but leave your family in New York even after you learn that you are branch manager, do you then remain "away from home"? One taxpayer tried something like that, and the court said that *he* had a home and his family had a home, and he wasn't away from his home so nothing was deductible. Some people, the court said, maintain two residences as a "personal preference," not for business reasons. If you maintain two homes because you like your children's school—too bad. Schooling is a personal, not a business, matter. Write your congressman.

For some people, the world is their home for tax purposes. A traveling salesman who never stayed in one place longer than 30 days was not allowed to deduct any traveling expenses. For him, home was wherever he happened to be at the time: How could he be away from it? The decision is not

so heartless. You cannot deduct the cost of food and housing at your home because these are personal expenses. For the traveling salesman, his food and lodging expenses were equally personal. If you're a traveling salesman, you want to be sure to have a permanent place somewhere, where you go from time to time to collect your mail, change your shirts, and get your car tuned.

Mixing Business with Pleasure

Sometimes when you travel on business you do things unrelated to business. Sometimes business and pleasure trips get mixed up altogether. Expenses for pleasure trips are not deductible, whether you travel as an employee or on your own business.

Suppose you fly from New York to Chicago on business for two days, finish your business in the afternoon of the second day, attend the White Sox-Yankee ball game that night, and then catch the last plane back to New York. The entire cost of the trip (except the cost of tickets to the game or other purely recreational activities) is deductible because the primary purpose of the trip was business.

Suppose going to the ball game forces you to stay over one more night and take a morning flight. Everything except the tickets should be deductible (although to deduct the hotel room for the second night, you may have to show that you were too tired to return home that night.) Suppose you conduct your business on Thursday and Friday, then stay through Sunday to see a three-game series. You can deduct the plane fare and the cost of the meals and lodging (to the extent not reimbursed) for Thursday night and possibly Friday night, but an alert IRS agent will say that, by Saturday, the trip was no longer primarily for business, and meals and lodging on Saturday and Sunday should not be deductible. If your office sends you to Chicago on Friday solely to deliver a package to the Chicago branch, and you stay for the three-

game series, you can deduct the air fare and you might get away with one night of meals and lodging.

If you go to Chicago to see the three-game series and drop in on the branch office Friday afternoon to say hello, you might be able to deduct the taxi fare to and from the office if you can show a business purpose in saying hello. Once the trip is primarily for pleasure, only expenses made solely for business reasons are deductible.

The above rules apply only to domestic travel. Special rules apply if you mix business and pleasure on travel abroad. If you spend more than a week outside the country, you have to allocate all unreimbursed traveling expenses between the time you spent on business and the time you spent having a good time. Notice how this is different from the domestic travel rule. With domestic travel you could deduct all your meals and lodging for a trip even if you spent a great deal of time sightseeing, so long as your primary purpose for traveling was a business purpose. However, if you travel abroad for longer than a week, you must show what portion of your time was spent on business and only that portion of your travel expenses is deductible. There is an exception to this allocation rule if you can show that you spent at least 75 percent of the time abroad in pursuit of your business. Where allocations are necessary, the IRS has long, involved rules for making them.

For those who travel with their wives, her traveling expenses are deductible only if she is there for your business reasons. If the company, in its generosity, reimburses you for her expenses, the reimbursement will be gross income to you and you cannot deduct her expenses unless she was there for a business purpose. The Walt Disney Company has a solution to that problem. The Disney Company is in the business of family entertainment. It has an image to protect as a "family-oriented" business and considers it *essential* for executives to travel with their wives on business trips to

enhance this family image. The IRS challenged the deductions for a Disney executive's wife because, as far as it could tell, all she did was attend social functions. A California federal court sent the IRS packing back to Washington.

Some taxpayers take their wives along on business not because she has any business to conduct, but because he needs her so that he can conduct the business. A taxpayer who was too sick to travel alone took his wife with him on business trips. The Tax Court in Washington, D.C., said that she went along for personal (medical) reasons, not for business reasons, and denied the deduction as a business expense. Another taxpayer in the same situation was allowed the deduction by a Central Tennessee federal court, but a third taxpayer lost on the same facts in a federal court in Oregon. This is another state trooper problem. The conclusion is that if you take your wife on business trips because of your health, her traveling expenses are deductible from gross income if you live in Central Tennessee.

Most taxpayers who take their wives along on business trips pay the additional expense themselves and then try to deduct it, saying that the wife was necessary for social functions with business colleagues, or for helping to arrange and keep pace with a busy schedule. It is probably not advisable to try that. For one thing, once the IRS agent knows that your wife was along, he starts to suspect that the trip was partly for pleasure, and he starts to ask questions about that. If you stayed over just for the ball game, you may lose a whole day's deductions. Once the agent decides she wasn't along for any business reason, he wants to know whether part of the cost of the hotel was for an additional person in the room, and which part of the cost of meals was for her, and how much of the taxi fare was for dropping her off somewhere before your meeting. You don't know the answers to these questions, and before long he's making allocations—*assuming* that half the cost of the room was because of her and that she ate half the food—all of it nondeductible because she wasn't there for business reasons in the first place. It is usually too hard to prove your wife was along for a business reason, and it is more important to keep careful records which allocate to your wife the smallest possible legitimate portion of your expenses. After all, she doesn't eat much, and that taxi never went out of its way to drop her off. Then, if the IRS agent asks if she was along, you can attack: "Oh, sure, but I already took out her expenses." He may forget the whole thing.

If you insist on taking your wife along and want to have a good chance of deducting her expenses, marry your secretary.

Traveling expenses are deductible only so long as they are not "lavish or extravagant under the circumstances." Not even the IRS is sure of what that means. You might get away with one night at "21," but you can't eat there every night.

The cost of first-class air travel is not lavish or extravagant, but the President and some senators would like to change that and allow a deduction only for the cost of coach fare on the same flight. Fortunately for the business traveler, he has a champion in Senator Russell Long, the chairman of the Senate Finance Committee (the tax-writing committee in the Senate). Witness the following debate between him and Senator Kennedy on the Senate floor:

> MR. KENNEDY. Mr. President, this amendment is a very simple, a very basic, and a very fundamental amendment. It attempts to in a preliminary way deal with a matter which is of considerable concern to the American people, and that is the issue of expense-account living. That has been troublesome to the American taxpayer for a number of years, and the problem is getting worse.
>
> The purpose of the amendment is to disallow as a deductible business expense the excess of commercial first-class air travel fare over coach fare; coach fare would remain deductible.
>
> MR. LONG. Mr. President, if this amendment is agreed to it will not just reduce the use of first class; it will abolish first class. There will not be any first-class seats for anyone to fly on. The business air-

planes have been cutting back on the first-class seats anyway because there have been better services provided for the coach passengers. As a result, Mr. President, if businessmen cannot deduct their expenses of going first class they will find it so much more expensive that there will be very little demand for first class and there just will not be any first class, so just forget about first class. This is an amendment seeking to abolish all first class because it would work out that way.

Some people are big. It just happens to be that way. Some people are 4 feet taller than I am. Some people are big and cannot fit very comfortably in the coach-type seats so they need a first-class seat. It is a matter of human kindness to have enough space so they can spread out, and they need to have it where they buy that much space so they have enough foot space.

I know when I travel I oftentimes go first class because my wife is like my mother used to be. She is always bringing along strawberries for someone. To have foot space we need first-class seats with all the baggage Mrs. Long tends to bring aboard when she gets on the airplane to bring something back for a friend or something for the children or one thing and another, and we need a little extra space.

Furthermore, Mr. President, if we are going to tell people that they cannot fly first class then we should go the rest of the way and tell them when they get there they cannot take a taxicab; they have to take the bus; when they get to the hotel they cannot take a big room, they have to take a small room; and when they desire a restaurant they cannot go to the good restaurants, they have to go to the McDonald's, and so forth. I do not have anything against McDonald's; I eat there a great deal, but the point is once in a while a person should have a freedom of choice.

Years from now, historians will conclude that first-class transportation expenses were deductible because of Mrs. Long's strawberries.

When you deduct unreimbursed traveling expenses (or when your employer has not made you account for your expenses), as when you deduct unreimbursed transportation expenses, you must account for these expenses on your return. But for traveling expenses the accounting requirements are more detailed. You must be able to substantiate each "element" of the travel expense. This means that you must prove the amount of the expense (by receipt or diary entry), the date of departure and the date of return of your trip and how much of your trip was for business purposes, and where you went and what the business purpose of your journey was. Also, each traveling expense must be accounted for separately, although you can aggregate expenses for meals and for incidental expenses, such as taxi fares or gas and oil. But you cannot say, "$800 for the trip to Chicago." For all lodging expenses, and for any other expenditure of $25 or more, you must have documentary evidence which complements your diary or journal, such as a receipt. One exception to the documentary evidence rule is for transportation where a receipt is not available, for example, a $30 taxi ride. The IRS has a publication describing its substantiation requirements for traveling expenses, and this publication should be read with care if traveling expenses are a big item on your tax return.

Entertainment Expenses

Entertainment expenses incurred by an employee which are reimbursed by his employer are theoretically deductible in determining the employee's adjusted gross income. Remember, you may deduct all *reimbursed* business expenses in determining adjusted gross income. As with other reimbursed expenses, however, you usually don't have to worry about entertainment expenses when you do your tax return. If your employer has you account to him for the entertainment expenses in a manner which meets the IRS requirements, and then reimburses you exactly, you can just forget about it. It is his problem.

What if you are not reimbursed by your employer for entertainment expenses? Well, we have said that only unreimbursed *transportation* and *travel* expenses could be deducted from gross income. We didn't say anything about entertainment expenses. In determining adjusted gross income, you cannot deduct entertainment expenses incurred for business reasons unless you own the business, are an outside salesman, or are reimbursed by your employer (in which case you usually forget the whole thing). If you are employed by someone else, and take a prospective client or customer to lunch and don't get reimbursed, the cost of the lunch is not deductible in determining adjusted gross income. (If you entertain while you are traveling, entertainment expenses still are not deductible in determining adjusted gross income.) Unreimbursed entertainment expenses might be deductible in determining *taxable* income, if you itemize deductions, but only if your employer expects you or requires you to entertain business colleagues, and doesn't reimburse you or doesn't fully reimburse you. If you are not expected or required to entertain, or if you take advantage of the zero bracket amount, unreimbursed entertainment expenses are not deductible.

Why are unreimbursed entertainment expenses deductible, if at all, only in determining taxable income? Probably because if Congress let everybody deduct unreimbursed entertainment expenses in determining adjusted gross income, everybody would do just that. Even people who took advantage of the zero bracket amount would knock $200 or $300 from their gross income every year as "unreimbursed entertainment expenses." The IRS would be overwhelmed trying to verify all those entertainment deductions—not only whether they were made, but whether they were required or expected to be made. By allowing a deduction for unreimbursed entertainment expenses only to people who itemize deductions, the Congress saves the IRS a lot of trouble, because less than 25 percent of all taxpayers itemize deductions. That's a little trick on the part of your Congress.

Therefore, for employees the entertainment deduction is

mostly a problem in the computation of taxable income—when they are not reimbursed. But for some employees, the entertainment expense can be a problem in determining adjusted gross income. This occurs because some employers do not require adequate substantiation of entertainment expenses. They just pay their employees additional compensation which is intended to cover expected entertainment costs. In these cases, entertainment expenses are deductible from gross income (to the extent that they are reimbursed) *if* the employee can substantiate them. Since the employer obviously does not have the information necessary to substantiate, the responsibility for accounting to the government is back with the employee. He must submit a statement with his return, showing that the reimbursement (or the extra compensation) which he received was offset by the entertainment expenses. And he must be prepared to show that the entertainment expenses were valid ones. If he cannot show that, the deductions for the entertainment expenses will be disallowed, and he will have additional taxable income from the extra compensation. So let us look at when entertainment expenses are valid expenses, and at how you prove that.

Obviously the deduction for entertainment expenses is a troublesome one, for the taxpayer and for the IRS. It is one thing to prove (or disprove) that you took a trip for a business purpose. It is quite another thing to prove (or disprove) that an entertainment expense was incurred for business reasons. You take a friend out on your boat, you claim you did it for business reasons, you take a deduction. How does the IRS prove that you didn't do it for business reasons?

It doesn't. You prove that you did.

Entertainment expenses related to business are deductible under the part of the Internal Revenue Code dealing with "Deductions for Individuals and Corporations." But there is another part of the Code that I haven't mentioned yet. That part is entitled "Items Not Deductible." One "item not deductible" is "Certain Entertainment Expenses." To figure out what is deductible under "Deductions" you have to know what is not deductible under "Items Not Deductible."

It is the "Items Not Deductible" part that places the burden of proof for entertainment expenses on you. An entertainment expense is not deductible unless the taxpayer *establishes* one of two things: that the expense was "directly related to the active conduct of his trade or business"; or that the expense was "associated" with the active conduct of his trade or business and the entertainment "directly preceded" or "directly followed" a "substantial and bona fide" business discussion. (These rules are somewhat relaxed for business meals, as we shall see.) How do you establish these things? It's not easy.

Consider first the kind of entertainment which you claim is "directly related" to the active conduct of your trade or business. You take a colleague out on your boat for a business meeting. You seek to deduct the cost of the gasoline, and the lunch and beverages you bring along. What must you show in order to be able to deduct these expenses?

First, you must show that when you took your colleague out on your boat you had "more than a general expectation of deriving some income or other business benefit at some indefinite time in the future." There should at least be a possible deal in the works.

Next, you must show that while on your boat you "actively engaged in a business meeting, a business negotiation" or some other actual business transaction (you didn't just go fishing). If you can't show that, you have to show that you would have done one of those things but for circumstances beyond your control. So if a Great White shark chews your boat in half, it's okay if you didn't get around to discussing business. However, if the Great White chewed you up as you were heading back to port, the IRS might expect that you would have already discussed any business you were going to discuss.

Next, you must show that, viewing the entire event as a business-entertainment combination, the principal aspect of the event was the active conduct of your business. You locked in your fishing poles and then spread out the blueprints. Note that this requirement might give you trouble if you went fishing for three days.

Finally, you must show that the expenses for entertainment were attributable to you and your business associate. That is not an absolute rule: You and your guest can bring your wives along, and you can deduct expenses attributable to them. But you can't treat the whole neighborhood on the federal treasury.

If you can't show all these things, then you can still claim the deduction if you show that the entertainment occurred in a "clear business setting directly in furtherance of" your trade or business. That may be hard to do with your boat, especially if nonbusiness colleagues are aboard. But this test might be helpful if your business was selling boats. Under this test you must always show that your guest should have known that your primary motive for entertaining him was to further your trade or business. So it is important to make it clear up front that you are going out on your boat to talk business, particularly where your business colleague is also a friend.

Suppose the entertainment is the kind "associated" with the active conduct of your trade or business and directly precedes or follows a "substantial and bona fide" business discussion—for example, a night at the ball game or the theater. Or an evening at a cabaret or even a sail on your boat where business is not discussed. To deduct the cost of this entertainment, you must show that the expenditure was made with a "clear business purpose," such as to obtain new business or maintain an existing business relationship. If a friend with whom you do no business is in town, and after remembering old times in your office you go to the ball game, it will be hard to show a clear business purpose.

When you are able to show that "clear business purpose," you must also show that the entertainment came just before or just after an active business negotiation or meeting or other good faith business transaction. When does entertainment occur "just before" or "just after"? You are usually safe if the business meeting and the entertainment occur on the same day. If they occur on separate days, you should have a reason why—for example, your business colleague arrived from out of town late in the day, you entertained him that night, and the next morning you got down to business.

How do you show all these things? You keep records, you dictate memoranda on what you talked about during or around the time of the entertainment, you write a letter to your guest which starts out, "During the discussion of the big contract on my boat on June 20 . . ." and more. The IRS has extensive substantiation requirements. As with travel expenses, each "element" of the expenditure must be substantiated. For entertainment expenses, the elements are: amount of each separate expenditure; aggregating incidental expenses such as taxis; time, place, and nature of the entertainment; its business purpose (what you expected to gain from it); and the business relationship between you and your guest. Where the entertainment is "associated" with your trade or business, you must substantiate, in addition to these elements, the time, place, and purpose of the business meeting which was held just before or just after the entertainment, and you must identify which of the people you entertained participated in the business meeting. If your brother-in-law was along for the ride, there will be no entertainment expense deduction for him.

The IRS also has rules on what constitutes "substantiation" for entertainment expenses. You must keep a diary or account book, or some kind of statement of expenses, which is prepared at about the same time as the expense is made, and for expenses of $25 or more, you must have receipts or other documentary evidence.

When we discussed entertaining people on your boat, we didn't mention deductions for the boat itself, such as maintenance, or docking fees. That is because the boat itself is considered an "entertainment facility." So is your cabin at the lake or the country club you belong to. Expenditures in connection with an entertainment facility are deductible to the extent that the facility is used for business, but only if the facility is used "primarily" in furtherance of your trade or business. That is usually a question of facts and circumstances, but you are safe if you can show that more than 50 percent of all use was in furtherance of your trade or business. For employees, that is usually difficult to prove.

The whole entertainment expense deduction is a minefield, and we have touched on only a few of the rules. You may want tax guidance if entertainment expenses are to be an important item on your return.

For business meals and drinks, you don't have to show a direct relationship to the active conduct of a trade or business, or even a "clear business setting." All you have to show to deduct the cost of a meal is that it occurred under circumstances "conducive to business discussions." That means that your luncheon guest was someone with whom you were likely to discuss business. You needn't have actually discussed it. However, you must have dined in a place where it was possible to discuss business. Floor shows and business meals do not mix, as far as the IRS is concerned. The substantiation requirements for business meals are basically the same as for other entertainment expenses: Substantiate each "element."

Once the IRS took a taxpayer to court and argued that for entertainment consisting of meals, the cost of the taxpayer's meal wasn't deductible. "He would have eaten anyway," the IRS argued, in effect.

The argument sounded pretty good to the Tax Court, but

it was a short-lived victory for the IRS. A sharp taxpayer has no trouble getting around that ruling. "I had yogurt and tea because I was on a diet. My guest had foie gras, a chateaubriand for two, melon (en saison), and a Pouilly Fuissé 1962, preceded by two glasses of Mandarine Napoleon and followed by a brandy which the maître d' had been keeping in the cellar since 1897." Or, "Normally I would have had yogurt and tea. So as not to make my guest uncomfortable, I had the New York strip and wine. The difference between the cost of the yogurt and tea and the cost of the steak and wine should be deductible."

IRS agents are not masochists. They don't want to listen to that day after day. The IRS has announced that it will deny the deduction for the taxpayer's meal only in "abusive" situations. Nobody is sure what that means.

During 1978, there was a brouhaha in Washington over the deductibility of entertainment expenses. The President described the "three-martini lunch" as a national disgrace and proposed to allow a deduction for only half of entertainment expenses for meals (which is all the IRS was trying to do). As for other entertainment expenses, such as a trip on your boat, they were to be disallowed altogether. Business people, restauranteurs, and even restaurant workers saw things differently. After much debate, Congress decided to repeal only the deduction for "entertainment facilities," the item which seldom affects individuals.

Education Expenses

Under the tax laws, education expenses are treated like entertainment expenses in that they are usually deductible from gross income only to the extent that they are reimbursed. If not reimbursed (and if otherwise allowable), they may be deducted only from adjusted gross income, and then only if you itemize deductions. We will look at education expenses at this point because, to be deductible at all, they must be related to your trade or business. Also, if you are reimbursed for education expenses which cannot be deducted, you will have income from the reimbursement which will be subject to tax.

When are education expenses "related" to your trade or business and therefore deductible? Let me first tell you when they are *not* deductible. They are not deductible when your studies will qualify you for a new trade or business, a new job or career. Even if you are not interested in finding a new career, the expenses are not deductible. After all, if your studies prepare you for a different trade or business, how can they be related only to your present one?

Education expenses are deductible under two circumstances: when your employer requires you to take certain studies in order to keep your present job; or when your studies improve your skills and help you do your present job better, even if they are not required by your employer. But if these studies will also qualify you for a new career, you get no deduction.

A good example of how the education-expense deduction rules are applied is as follows (the example is even used, in part, by the IRS). Suppose you work in a bank as a trust officer, and you are required by your employer to obtain a law degree. Since your employer requires you to obtain the degree it would seem that the education expenses would be deductible. Even if he did not require it, having a law degree would improve your skills as a trust officer. Nonetheless, the expense of getting a law degree would not be deductible because having a law degree would also enable you to enter a new career—as a lawyer. Even if you didn't want to practice law, even if you hated lawyers, you would be stuck with the fact that you could be a lawyer, and your education expenses would not be deductible. If the bank paid for your education, you would have additional income.

Suppose the bank does not require a law degree, but only requires that you take some courses in taxes and estates.

Well, taking a few law courses in taxes and estates would not qualify you for a new trade or business, so then the education expenses would be deductible, either because the courses would help you to do your job better or because your employer requires you to take the courses to retain your job. But if you become enthusiastic and decide to enter into a curriculum at law school which *could* lead to a degree in law (no matter how long it would take), then you would lose the deduction.

Note that the fact that your studies could result in a degree is not determinative. What matters is whether they prepare you for a new career—with or without a degree. For example, many lawyers obtain master's degrees in tax law or labor law while they are practicing law. Their studies lead to a degree but do not qualify them for a new career. These studies just help them to perform their present jobs better, and their education expenses are deductible.

Obviously the big problem with the education-expense deduction is in determining whether your studies qualify you for a "new trade or business." Sometimes it is clear that they do or do not—as with our trust officer or lawyer. Sometimes it is not so clear. The IRS says that, for employees, "A change of duties does not constitute a new trade or business if the new duties involve the same general type of work as is involved in the individual's present employment." As an example it gives a change from a classroom teacher to a principal—so expenses for studies necessary to make that change are deductible. A Tax Court has said that a new trade or business is one which is "substantially" different from that in which you are presently employed. Within these broad guidelines, each case turns on its own facts.

Sometimes you will obtain a temporary job which will become permanent once you take certain courses you need in order to qualify for the job. Educational expenses incurred under these circumstances are not deductible. Even though you have the job already, you do not become qualified for it until you take those courses. Expenses for studies which enable you to meet the minimum educational requirements of your employment are never deductible. However, if the minimum requirements change after you meet them once, then additional studies would be required by your employer and the cost of the studies would be deductible.

At the beginning of this discussion we said that unreimbursed education expenses are usually deductible only from adjusted gross income. But sometimes education expenses will include transportation or travel expenses, such as automobile or taxi expenses to and from school, or even meals and lodging if your school is far enough away. We have seen that transportation and travel expenses, if related to your trade or business, are deductible from gross income. The result is that if your underlying education expenses (tuition, books, lab fees) are related to your trade or business and deductible from adjusted gross income, the related expenses for travel and transportation are deductible from gross income. This fact might be important if you do not itemize deductions and if your underlying education expenses are not substantial enough to make you itemize. You could still deduct the travel and transportation costs from gross income.

What if your education consists mostly of traveling? As long as it improves your skills or is required by your employer (and does not prepare you for a new career), the expenses are all deductible. The classic example is the French teacher on a sabbatical who travels throughout France, visiting French schools and going to movies, plays, and lectures in the French language, all intended to improve her French language skills, and all deductible.

Moving Expenses

Moving expenses may seem personal in nature but Congress has found that in this country moving is a cost of earning money. Congress also thinks that a mobile labor force is important to the economy. Consequently, moving expenses, if deductible, are always deductible in determining adjusted gross income.

To be able to deduct moving expenses at all, you must move because you have a new "principal place of work"— a new office or a new job. After you arrive in your new home, you must work at a full-time job during thirty-nine weeks of the next year. So there are no deductions for transients. (The thirty-nine-week rule does not apply if you are fired.) If you are self-employed, you must pursue a full-time occupation for at least thirty-nine weeks in the next year, and at least seventy-eight weeks total over two years. There are no deductions for enterprising transients. If these length-of-stay requirements are not met when it comes time to file your tax return, the government gives you the benefit of the doubt. But if you claim the deduction and then fail to stay long enough, the amount of the deduction is income in the following year.

In addition, your new place of work cannot be too near your old house. It must be at least 35 miles farther from your old house than your old place of work was. Under the 35-mile rule, if your old office was 10 miles from the house on Chestnut Street, your new office must be at least 45 miles from the Chestnut Street house if you want a deduction for moving expenses. If the new office is 44 miles from Chestnut Street, you get no deduction for moving closer to the new office. Congress figures if you drove 10 miles to get to work before, you can drive 44 miles now (the rule was 50 miles, not 35, before the Arab oil embargo). If your old office was 40 miles from Chestnut Street, the new office must be at least 75 miles from Chestnut Street if you want a deduction for moving closer to it. The reason for the 35-mile rule is to disallow moving-expense deductions to people who just move from one house to another one in the same town after they change jobs or their office moves across the street. But why Congress feels that people who drove 10 miles before can drive 45 miles now is a mystery to me.

The 35 miles is measured by the most direct route which people in the area commonly travel. Shortcuts don't count, and you are not expected to fly in a straight line.

Deductible moving expenses include the cost of moving your furniture and other belongings, and yourself (transportation, meals, and lodging) from the old house to the new house. You can deduct these expenses, as long as they are reasonable, regardless of the amount.

You can also deduct expenses incurred for traveling to your new town to look for a house, and the cost of renting a place while you are waiting to move into your new house. But for these expenses there are limits. For one thing, you can deduct the cost of temporary living quarters only for thirty consecutive days. After that, the cost of temporary living quarters is not deductible. In any event, the most you can deduct for the expense of searching for your new place and for the cost of temporary living quarters is $1500. The reason for these limitations will become obvious to you later on in the book. For a high-bracket taxpayer, it might be worth his while to live in expensive temporary quarters and "look" for a new place forever if these costs were fully deductible. Say you are in the 40 percent tax bracket. You are prepared to spend $600 per month on an apartment in your new town. If your temporary living costs are deductible, you can afford to pay $1000 per month—because the $1000 monthly deduction saves you $400 in taxes. So if you like your $1000 place, you might keep "looking" indefinitely.

You can also deduct costs incurred in selling your old house or getting out of a lease, or in buying your new house or paying someone to get out before his lease expires. Expenses of selling or buying a house include broker's or finder's fees, attorney's fees, appraisal fees, transfer taxes, and closing costs (but not fixing-up expenses). The amount of these expenses which is deductible is limited to $3000. In addition, the $3000 limitation is reduced by any deductions allowed for finding a new place or for temporary living quarters while waiting to move in. If you deduct $1200 for house-searching and temporary living quarters, the most you can deduct for selling or buying costs is $1800.

If your employer reimburses you for your moving expenses—you guessed it—it's income to you.

There are other "business-like" expenses for people who don't own a trade or business. For example, there is a deduction for the amount of interest that you lose when you prematurely withdraw your savings from a time deposit. You promise to leave $1000 in your savings bank for a year and so the bank pays you a higher interest rate, and then you withdraw it three days later and so the bank penalizes you for that. The penalty is deductible in determining adjusted gross income. It is an expense of producing income.

Some deductions from gross income are not very "business-like" at all—alimony payments, for example. They are deductible in determining adjusted gross income even though they are not business expenses. As we saw earlier, amounts paid to a former spouse which are included in her gross income are deductible from your gross income. But you don't get a deduction if she doesn't take the payment into income—as with a lump-sum settlement. Up until 1976, alimony payments could be deducted only if you itemized deductions. But so many voters get divorced, including lower income voters who don't itemize, that Congress made it a deduction for everybody.

There is also a deduction from gross income for amounts you contribute to an "individual retirement account" or to an "individual retirement annuity." These are the government-approved, personal pension plans for people. You see your banker or insurance company about setting up one of these plans. Once you set it up, you can make contributions toward your retirement—as much as 15 percent of your earned income (but usually no more than $1500) per year— and take a deduction for the contributions. We will talk more about individual retirement accounts in Chapter 13.

If you own a trade or business, you know that there are many more business deductions which you can take in determining your adjusted gross income—deductions such as interest payments, tax payments, charitable contributions, certain losses, and so on. All these deductions can also be claimed by everybody who itemizes deductions, and so they will be discussed in the next chapter. Capital losses can also be deducted in determining adjusted gross income, but we'll talk about them when we get to capital gains. There are also a number of deductions from gross income connected with corporate pension plans—but that gets much too technical for this book. (There are tax lawyers whose practice is devoted solely to the tax aspects of pensions.)

That winds up the calculation of adjusted gross income. To sum up: At this point you have added up all the income that you made and reduced it by the money you spent to make it. You might say that you have determined your "net gross income." (But you don't say that; you say you have determined your "adjusted gross income.") Now you are ready to determine your taxable income. Once you know your taxable income, you do some multiplying and you come up with your tax. And then you pay your tax—unless you can figure out a way to reduce your taxes to zero or to avoid incurring any tax liability in the first place. After we see how to figure out your taxable income, we'll get to the question of not paying taxes in any event.

SIX
Taxable Income, or the Great American Deduction

Taxable income is the income you pay tax on. It is adjusted gross income reduced by further deductions. Most deductions that reduce adjusted gross income to taxable income are not business deductions. They are personal deductions, and not amounts spent to produce income. These are amounts spent to *live*.

What amounts spent to live are deductible? At first glance the answer appears to be: *No* amounts. *None.* Nothing. Section 262 of the Code says, *"No* deduction shall be allowed for personal, living, or family expenses." Just as *everything* is income, *nothing* is deductible. Unless . . . Unless the Code says it's deductible. Here again is our old friend "Except as otherwise provided." Section 262 says no personal deduction shall be allowed *"Except as otherwise expressly provided."* Elsewhere, it is expressly provided otherwise. We are about to go through all the deductions for personal, living, and family expenses. At the end, you may say, "But what about . . . ?" Forget it. If the Code doesn't specifically say it's deductible, it's not deductible, period.

There are two ways to reduce adjusted gross income by personal expenses: One way is to use the "zero bracket amount," which used to be called the "standard deduction" and the other way is to "itemize" deductions.

The "zero bracket amount" is simple. It is a flat amount of money by which your adjusted gross income is automatically reduced when figuring your tax. If you are married and file a joint return for 1978, your adjusted gross income is automatically reduced by $3200 (if you are single, $2200). That is your "zero bracket amount." You automatically get a $3200 (or $2200) deduction. No questions asked. (For 1979, the "zero bracket amount" is $3400 for married people filing jointly, and $2300 for single people.)

The "zero bracket amount" was once called the "standard deduction." Instead of being a flat amount ($3200 or $2200) it used to be *either* a percentage of your adjusted gross income *or* a flat amount, whichever was smaller. And instead of getting the deduction automatically when you figured out your tax, you had to go through the mechanics of subtracting the smaller amount from your adjusted gross income. But in 1977 Congress decided to give all married people a flat standard deduction of $3200, and all single people a flat standard deduction of $2200. Once the standard deduction became a fixed amount, it was no longer necessary to make you go through the motion of subtracting it from your adjusted gross income—because the standard deduction would always be the same amount for each category of taxpayer. So Congress just built the standard deduction into the tax-rate schedule and the tax tables. Today, when you go to figure out your tax, the standard deduction is already accounted for. The rate schedule or tax tables automatically reduce your adjusted gross income by the zero bracket amount.

Is it to your advantage to take a deduction for your personal expenses by using the zero bracket amount? Maybe yes. Maybe no. Read on and examine the alternative.

The alternative is to itemize your deductions. There are certain personal (as opposed to business) expenditures which the Congress says, for one reason or another, can be subtracted from adjusted gross income to determine taxable income. Not just any item that may seem indispensable to you just to stay alive. Only certain items, specifically named, that Congress says you can deduct, provided you itemize deductions.

For individual taxpayers, as of this writing, there are over thirty deductible items. But when we speak of "itemized deductions," we are usually referring only to five or six of these deductions. Most of the deductible items are business-related and may be deducted from gross income (such as travel expenses, or moving expenses). Only five or six of the deductible items are for *personal* expenses which may be deducted from adjusted gross income and which we call the "itemized deductions." These itemized deductions are (1) the "medical-expense" deduction, (2) state and local tax deductions, (3) deductions for losses of property from fire, theft, or other "casualties," (4) deductions for charitable contributions, and (5) "interest" deductions (amounts you pay in interest on loans). A sixth expense, for political contributions, can be claimed either as a deduction or as a tax credit, and we shall examine that expense in Chapter 9.

Sometimes you add up your itemized deductions and find that they total less than $3200 (or $2200 if you are single). Then you just take advantage of the zero bracket amount. You're ahead of the game. Or maybe you don't want to bother keeping track of all your deductible expenses or adding them up. Use the zero bracket amount. In permitting an "automatic deduction" under the zero bracket amount procedure, Congress has said, in effect: "Look, we let you reduce your adjusted gross income by all these itemized deductions—all these special amounts you spend. But we figure that, for most people, these amounts don't add up to more than $3200 for two people —or to more than $2200 for single people. So to save everyone—you and the IRS—a lot of trouble, if you want to do it this way, we'll let you skip all the records and the figuring. You can just use the zero bracket amount which automatically reduces your adjusted gross income, and forget the whole thing."

For most people what Congress says is true. For at least 75 percent of the people, the zero bracket amount is a simple, adequate substitute for adding up all those itemized deductions. But not for all people.

What's Your Tax Bracket?

To understand why some people reject the easier course, you have to understand the tax rates. The United States income tax is a "progressive" tax. High income, high taxes —not only because of more income to be taxed, but also because under a "progressive" tax system, as your income climbs, it gets taxed at a higher rate.

Consider these rates on taxable income in 1978 for married couples:

The first $3200 is not taxed at all (because under the zero bracket amount procedure, that amount of income is treated as zero income).

The next $1000 is taxed at 14 percent.

The next $1000, at 15 percent.

And up it goes. For example:

Taxable income in excess of $15,200—25 percent.

Taxable income in excess of $23,200—32 percent.

Taxable income in excess of $47,200—50 percent.

That is a progressive tax—as you add to your income, the government takes a greater part of the *addition*. It doesn't sound very progressive, does it?

For 1979, the Congress has lowered the tax rates by reducing some of the percentages and widening the brackets to which they apply. Further cuts may come later. The Congress raises or lowers the tax rates every few years. But the tax system is still a progressive tax.

One point should be made clear about these escalating rates, which are called "tax brackets." We have all heard people say, "I'm in the 25 percent bracket" or "I'm in the 50 percent bracket." But being in the 50 percent bracket doesn't mean that half your taxable income goes to taxes. It means that half your taxable income in excess of $47,200 goes to taxes. Your first $1000 in excess of $3200 is still taxed at 14 percent. The next $1000 at 15 percent. If you file a joint return showing taxable income of $47,201 your precise tax would be $14,060.50—which is calculated at gradually increasing rates from the first $3200 right on up. Actually, it figures out to be about 30 percent of the whole $47,201, not 50 percent. On anything *over* $47,200 you pay tax at the rate of 50 percent. So of that $47,201 of income, only one dollar is taxed at the 50 percent rate. The rate of tax on your top dollars of income—the highest rate at which a portion of your income is taxed—is referred to as your "marginal" rate of tax or your "marginal bracket."

When people say, "I don't need any more income this year because it will just push me into a higher tax bracket," they probably don't understand the tax system. On an overall basis, getting "pushed into a higher tax bracket" doesn't cost you much more in tax. That first $1000 in excess of $3200 is still taxed at 14 percent, whatever "marginal bracket" you're in. If your taxable income is $31,200, you are in the "39 percent bracket." If your taxable income is $31,-201, you enter the "42 percent bracket." Does this mean a difference of 3 percent in overall tax? Not at all. With a taxable income of $31,200, your tax is exactly $7100. With a taxable income of $31,201, your tax is exactly $7100.42. Overall, there has been little change. On your income from $27,201 to $31,200, you pay tax at the 39 percent rate. On the first dollar over $31,200, you pay at the 42 percent rate. Getting pushed into a higher bracket doesn't increase your tax liability by 3 percent overall. It increases it by .006 of 1 percent, and then only because the top $1 of your taxable income is taxed at 42 percent instead of at 39 percent. Knowledgeable people who say "No more income this year" are thinking that they prefer to take the income next year, because next year they think they will have less income and be in a lower marginal bracket. They hope that the income they turn their backs on this year will be taxed at a lower rate next year. But they do not mean that they never want the income.

By the same token, getting yourself into a lower tax bracket doesn't save you much tax on an overall basis either. Lowering your bracket saves you no more tax overall than raising your bracket costs you. Deductions are not used primarily to get yourself into a lower tax bracket. A $1 deduction from a taxable income of $31,201 drops you into a 3 percent lower tax bracket, but saves you only 42 cents in tax.

Nonetheless, because of the progressive tax system, the $1 deduction is worth more to someone in a higher tax bracket. For a married man with $50,000 of taxable income, all of his income from $47,201 to $50,000 is taxed at the 50 percent rate. For each dollar by which he reduces his taxable income, he pays 50 cents less in tax. A married man with $15,000 of taxable income pays tax at a lower rate. All his income from $11,201 to $15,000 is taxed at the 22 percent rate. So each dollar of deduction saves him only 22 cents in tax. The one dollar deduction is worth 28 cents more to the richer man.

Neither the richer man nor the poorer man would throw his money away just to get a deduction. If throwing your money away would reduce your overall tax liability right down to the first dollar of income by, say, 3 percent, of course you might do it. But, as we have seen, it doesn't work that way. The important thing about the progressive tax system is that it makes it easier for the richer man to throw away a dollar. Suppose you got a deduction for throwing your money off a bridge. If you have taxable income of $15,000 there is no point in throwing a dollar off a bridge just to reduce your tax liability by 22 cents. You would still lose 78 cents. On the other hand, if you have taxable income of $50,000 and you throw a dollar off the bridge, you've only lost 50 cents. You reduce your taxes by 50 cents and you throw away 50 cents you would otherwise keep.

But these itemized deductions are not like money you throw off a bridge. They are usually amounts that you would spend anyway. So if you would spend it anyway, why not reduce your taxes by listing it? That is what these itemized deductions let you do.

Medical Expenses

For example, take *medical-expense* deductions. Medical expenses are practically all expenses related to your health —expenses for doctors, dentists, optometrists, therapists, hospitalization, wheelchairs, drugs, even medical insurance, and more. Congress lets you take a deduction for a certain part of these medical expenses. Not all of them, but only that portion in excess of a certain amount.

The calculation of the medical-expense deduction has always been one of the more complicated calculations in the Code. An attempt to simplify it was made in 1978, but without success. To demonstrate what the Congress had to work with, we will find our way through the calculation, step by step, and then look at the somewhat simpler version of the medical-expense deduction which was proposed.

This is how the Code explains the medical-expense deduction (are you ready for this?):

(a) There shall be allowed as a deduction the following amounts, not compensated by insurance or otherwise—

(1) the amount by which the amount of the expenses paid during the year (reduced by any amount deductible under paragraph (2)) for medical care of the taxpayer, his spouse and dependents (as defined in section 152) exceeds 3 percent of his adjusted gross income, and

(2) an amount (not in excess of $150) equal to one-half of the expenses paid during the taxable year for insurance which constitutes medical care for the taxpayer, his spouse and dependents.

(b) Amounts paid during the taxable year for medicine and drugs which (but for this subsection) would be taken into account in computing the deduction under subsection (a) shall be taken into account only to the extent that the aggregate of such amounts exceeds 1 percent of the adjusted gross income.

Calculating the medical-expense deduction is simpler if viewed as follows.

Start with your medical insurance premiums. If you itemize deductions, 50 percent of your medical insurance premiums are automatically deductible—but only up to $150. If you paid $490 in insurance premiums, you can deduct, not $245, but only $150. So you take that deduction. It's yours, whatever else happens.

Now imagine that you have a big pot and you are throwing medical expenses into the pot. The first thing you put in the pot is the remaining $340 in medical insurance premiums that you couldn't deduct automatically. Next, you throw all your other medical expenses into the pot, except your expenses for medicine and drugs. You throw in doctors bills, hospital bills, wheelchair bills—everything except bills for drugs or medicine. Suppose all those doctors bills, etc., come to $700. Adding that to the $340 in medical insurance premiums you threw in first, you have $1040 in the big pot. Let's call these your "big pot medical expenses."

Next to the big pot you have a small pot. Into the small pot you throw all your bills for drugs and medicine. Let us say they come to $280.

Now you look at your adjusted gross income. Suppose it is $23,000. You take 1 percent of it: $230. Then go to the small pot. Expenses for medicine and drugs (in this case $280) in excess of 1 percent of your adjusted gross income (in this case $230) are eligible for being deducted. So you have $50 in eligible medicine and drug expenses. You take the $50 in eligible medicine and drug expenses and you throw it into the big pot, and they become "big pot medical expenses."

Now you look at the big pot again. There is $1090 in "big pot medical expenses" in it—$1040 from doctors bills and insurance premiums, and $50 in drugs. "Big pot medical expenses," including medical insurance premiums not automatically deductible (premiums above that first $150 that I said was yours) and also including eligible medicine and drug expenses (that $50 that came out of the small pot) are deductible to the extent that they exceed 3 percent of your adjusted gross income. Three percent of your adjusted gross income of $23,000 is $690. "Big pot medical expenses" in excess of that are deductible. You have $1090 in medical expenses in the big pot. So $400 is the deductible amount.

Your total medical-expense deductions, then, are $400 from the big pot plus $150 in medical insurance premiums (the part we set aside first). Total: $550.

Rephrasing the Code language quoted above: You can always deduct 50 percent of medical insurance premiums up to $150. You can deduct all other medical expenses, including the nondeducted part of medical insurance premiums, to the extent that they exceed 3 percent of your adjusted gross income, but in totaling your medical expenses you can only count expenses for drugs and medicine that are in excess of 1 percent of your adjusted gross income.

The President thought that this medical-expense computation was a little complicated. I can't imagine why. He wanted to throw out the special rules for medical insurance and drugs, and raise the 3 percent floor to 10 percent. You would have just added up all your medical expenses. If they exceeded 10 percent of your adjusted gross income, you would have deducted the excess. For our taxpayer with $23,000 of adjusted gross income, that would have put an end to the medical-expense deduction, since his total medical expenses ($1470) would not have exceeded 10 percent of his adjusted gross income ($2300). The House was unwilling to go along. "We're for simplification," it said, "but not for reducing the amount of the deduction by so much." So the House, like the President, proposed that all medical expenses be added up, but that the three-percent floor be retained. The Senate would not even agree to that. Why? Because most people claim only the $150 deduction for medical insurance; their other medical expenses seldom exceed three percent of their adjusted gross income. The Senate wanted to preserve that automatic deduction. So the law remains unchanged. Sometimes "simplification" must yield to tax breaks that benefit so many people.

Why does the government let you deduct medical expenses? The medical-expense deduction was added to the Code in 1942, during World War II, "in consideration of the heavy tax burden that must be borne by individuals during the existing emergency and of the desirability of maintaining the present high level of public health and morale." What a magnificent justification: the "public morale." It would be great for the "public morale" if they canceled the income tax altogether for a year or two.

Today the government says you can deduct medical expenses because it wants you to seek medical help when you need it, and it wants you to have medical insurance. But the fact is, once Congress writes a deduction, it's hard to get rid of it.

Why doesn't the government let you deduct all your medical expenses and insurance premiums, and avoid the complicated calculations? For one thing, the government figures it shouldn't subsidize health insurance. That's why some health insurance premiums are not automatically deductible. You can't deduct all your other medical expenses because the medical-expense deduction is designed to relieve hardship. The government figures everybody has to spend a certain amount of money on their health anyway. If you have a headache, you may buy some aspirin. If you have a toothache, you go to the dentist. That doesn't kill you financially. Medical expenses hurt only if you have a major illness or accident—something that doesn't happen to most people, and that you may not be equipped financially to handle. The government still wants you to have the medical attention you need—so it helps you out by reducing your taxes somewhat.

Sometimes the medical-expense deduction will carry you a long way. Nothing the President wants would change that. You'd be amazed at what can constitute a medical expense. The cost of a legal abortion is a qualifying medical expense. As is the cost of prescribed birth-control methods. If you park your car in a garage when you visit your doctor, the cost of parking the car is a medical expense. So is the cost of the gasoline and tolls. The government even gives you 7 cents a mile for wear and tear. If you must fly to a distant city to see a specialist, the travel expenses are medical expenses. If your doctor orders you to spend two weeks in Arizona after your lung operation, the cost of transportation (but not food and lodging) is a medical expense. For any expense to be a medical expense, it must be made to relieve or prevent a medical disorder. So you do not incur any medical expenses if you just go to Arizona "for your health." And the cost of those vitamins you pop every day would normally be a medical expense only if prescribed by a doctor.

If you put an elevator in your house so that a disabled family member can get upstairs you have an eligible medical expense—but only to the extent that the elevator does not increase the value of the house. Suppose you pay $5000 for the elevator, but installing it increases the value of the house by $3000. You have a qualifying medical expense of $2000. One woman was ordered by her doctor to swim every day as therapy to prevent paralysis from a spinal injury. If she'd joined a pool club for $200 per year, that would have been a medical expense. Instead, she built a swimming pool for $194,000. She figured that the value of her house was increased by $86,000. The cost included $26,000 in expenses for landscaping not essential to her having a pool. That left $82,000 in "medical expenses." The IRS flipped, but the Court said that almost all of it was deductible. (Part of the $82,000 included the cost of imported tile. The Court felt that imported tile was not necessary for medicinal purposes.)

Obviously, if your medical expenses are covered by medical insurance, you don't need the government's help, and covered expenses are not deductible. However, medical insurance seldom pays for your pool.

How much does the government really help you by letting you deduct extraordinary medical expenses? In the calculation above, in which your medical expenses went into a big pot, you had $550 in deductible medical expenses and an adjusted gross income of $23,000. At that level in 1978 your top income is taxed at 28 percent (if you are married). For every dollar you reduce your income, you save 28 cents in tax. By having $550 in medical-expense deductions, you reduce your taxes by $154. In effect, the government pays you $154 just for spending money you would have spent anyway. The numbers might be changing but not the underlying principle.

Notice that if medical expenses were the only deduction you had, they wouldn't do you much good. You are better off taking advantage of the zero bracket amount. With an adjusted gross income of $23,000, the zero bracket amount of $3200 reduces your taxes by $896 instead of $154. But you are likely to have other deductions.

Taxes

Do you live in a state with an income tax? If you live in New York City, you live in a city with an income tax and in a state with an income tax. Those income taxes that you pay to your local government are all deductible, if you itemize deductions. And well they should be. You never have a right to the money you pay to your city or state as income taxes. You never even see it if your employer withholds it. And people living in states without income taxes start off with more spendable income than you, so at tax time the deduction helps you catch up by reducing your federal taxes.

Many state or local taxes, besides income taxes, are deductible. (Federal taxes never are.) If you own a decent car, you probably pay another tax—the personal property tax. This tax is deductible as well—so long as it is based on the value of your property and not just a flat registration fee. Your real estate taxes are also deductible.

State taxes on gasoline are deductible for 1978, but not for 1979. The government will no longer subsidize the use of gasoline, so we won't count that deduction.

If you have adjusted gross income of $20,000 per year, you probably pay $1000 per year in state income taxes and $100 per year in personal property taxes.

You probably pay $300 per year in general sales taxes. Every time the man rings up the cash register, you pay another few cents in sales tax. Any "general" sales tax may also be deducted. A "general" sales tax is one that applies to a broad range of items, usually at the same rate. If you buy a new car, you may pay several thousand cents in sales tax. Do you have to keep track of all these cents? Of course not. The government gives you a table which tells you about how much you pay in sales taxes every year, depending on how much you make and which state you live in. If you haven't kept records, you can use the tables. In fact, if you've kept records for certain big items—a car, a boat, an airplane, or a home (including a mobile home and materials to build a home), you can add the sales tax on those items to the sales tax in the tables and deduct the whole thing. (But you should keep records. Unless you are very frugal, you'll always come out ahead of the government's tables.)

Add up all these nonfederal taxes you've paid—$1000 in state income taxes, $300 in general sales taxes, $100 in personal property taxes. You have another $1400 in deductions. (I have left out city taxes because only a few cities have an income tax. If you live in one, you add that in too.) Plus your $550 in medical-expense deductions. Now you have $1950 in deductions. At the 28 percent bracket ($23,000 income level), they are worth a tax savings of $546. The government has reduced your taxes by $546 because you spent money that you would have spent anyway. Nonetheless, the $3200 zero bracket amount, worth $896 at this bracket, is still a better deal.

In 1978, the President proposed to disallow the deductions for personal property taxes and sales taxes. This was intended to help simplify the tax laws. But the Congress didn't see what was so complicated about these deductions and refused to go along. They are still in the law.

Casualty Losses

Another deduction allowable to taxpayers who itemize deductions is "losses of property" arising from "fire, storm, shipwreck, or other casualty, or theft." For example, if you have an automobile accident causing $200 damage, and you don't have insurance, you have a deduction arising from the accident. It's a "casualty loss."

The original congressional justification for the allowance of the casualty-loss deduction is obscure. Obviously, like the medical-expense deduction, it is designed to relieve hardship. The casualty-loss deduction is one of the oldest deductions in the tax laws. It first appeared in 1865—perhaps a year of great casualty, fire, and theft.

Under the casualty-loss deduction, if you have a $200 accident with your car, you cannot deduct the whole $200. That is because, for nonbusiness taxpayers, the first $100 of casualty losses is nondeductible. It is "nondeductible" for each accident. If you go out next week and do it again, the first $100 in losses in that accident is nondeductible too. If you have insurance and you collect from your insurance company, obviously you cannot deduct whatever you collect. (Also, it is the position of the IRS that if you could have collected from your insurer, but declined to do so, you cannot deduct what you could have collected.) What usually happens when you have a $200 accident is the insurance company pays you $100 because there is a $100 "deductible" clause in the insurance contract, and then you can't deduct the other $100 because there is a $100 "nondeductible" clause in the tax law.

When your property is damaged, how do you know how much of a deduction to claim? There is a two-part rule for determining the amount of the deduction. The first part states that the amount of the loss is measured by the decline in fair market value—the difference between the fair market values of the property before and after the casualty. This difference can usually be measured by the cost of repairs, and if the casualty is repairable, the allowable deduction is usually the cost of repairs (less $100). But the repairs can only give back to the property the value it had before the wreck. If hoodlums in your neighborhood smash all the manually operated windows in your car, you can't deduct the full cost of replacing them with power windows, but only the cost of new manual windows, installed. Also, if the cost of restoring the property to its original condition is greater than the decline in fair market value, you can deduct only the smaller figure.

If the property is totally destroyed, you never get to deduct its replacement value. The two-part rule in its entirety is that the amount deductible is one of two figures, whichever is lower: (1) the decline in fair market value, or (2) the property's "basis," which is usually its cost to you. This rule gets you going and coming. If the property destroyed is property which has decreased in value since you bought it, like a car, you can deduct only its fair market value just before the accident occurred (the "decline" in value for destroyed property being simply its precasualty value). If the property has increased in value over its cost, like a house, you can deduct only what you paid for it. In the tax law, this approach is called a "whipsaw."

In 1978, the President tried to change the casualty-loss deduction. He proposed that, instead of deducting casualty losses of more than $100, people add their casualty losses to their medical-expense deductions. Add all your bad luck together. The total of your "catastrophe" expenses was to be deductible to the extent that it exceeded 10 percent of adjusted gross income. He may try for that again in 1979. The change would be one of numbers only. You would still have to know whether you had a casualty loss. Sometimes that is not so easy to determine.

As a general rule, for a casualty loss, the event which results in the damage has to be of a "sudden, unexpected or unusual nature." It's easiest to get the deduction if the casualty is sudden. A flood, hurricane, lightning, or earthquake which destroys your property clearly results in a casualty loss. Without suddenness, you must rely on the "unexpected" or "unusual" test. A long, unusually cold winter which slowly freezes the pipes in your house may give rise to a casualty loss, but in a case like that it helps if you live in the South, so that your argument that the event was "unexpected" or "unusual" will be stronger.

Losses are not deductible if they are the result of "progressive deterioration." If the basement wall in your house starts to crack up because of poor drainage around it, no casualty loss will be allowed. People are always trying to deduct mechanical repairs to their cars (alleging flying rocks in the road, overloading, and potholes), and they are always losing because cars tend to deteriorate progressively. When the existence of deterioration is possible, it helps to have "an invasion by a hostile force" (to quote the IRS). Ordinary damage to trees or plants caused by insects won't get you a casualty-loss deduction. However, in one case, a taxpayer showed that his property suffered a "mass attack" by southern pine beetles which can destroy a tree in less than a week, and he was allowed the deduction.

Any loss has to be the direct result of the casualty. A taxpayer who was reimbursed by the insurance company for fire damage to his house tried to take a deduction for the "lost value" based on the resistance of people to buy a house which had caught fire. He lost. Another taxpayer who sold his beach house for less than he thought it was worth tried to deduct the difference, arguing that unusually bad storms that year had scared people away. The storms may have been unusual, but they didn't cause the loss directly.

Sometimes you can't even be sure if the event is sudden, unexpected, or unusual. In one case, a woman left her rings rolled up in tissue paper, and the next morning her husband promptly flushed them down the toilet. The court didn't think that that was so sudden, unexpected, or unusual. However, another taxpayer was allowed a deduction after he poured a glass of ammonia containing his wife's diamond ring down the sink and turned on the disposal. Maybe that is more unusual, or maybe the action of a disposal is more "sudden," or maybe it's just two courts interpreting the law differently. When another woman left her rings on the windowsill and the maid knocked them out the window, a casualty was found to have occurred. But a lady whose cat knocked over her expensive vase got nowhere when she tried to show that the cat was having an "unusual" nervous fit, rather than just behaving normally.

Theft losses are deductible in the same manner as casualty losses—the change in fair market value or the cost to you, whichever is lower. (When something is stolen, its value to you after the theft is zero, so the difference in fair market values before and after the loss is simply its pre-loss fair market value.) Again, the first $100 is not deductible. (The President would consider a theft loss a "catastrophe" deduction too.) You don't have to have a hard-core theft to get a deduction. Losses occurring from embezzlement or fraud are deductible as theft losses. Sometimes with embezzlement or fraud you don't even know there's been a theft until long after it occurs. That's okay—you take the deduction in whatever year you discover the loss. One taxpayer came home from a New Year's Eve party to discover $5000 in cash stolen. It was already January 1. He had to wait a whole year before he could claim the deduction.

You can't take a theft-loss deduction if you recover the property, or if there is a reasonable chance that you will recover it, or if you are compensated by insurance. If the police capture the thief and are holding your property as evidence, there's no theft loss.

Most important, there has to be a real theft. One taxpayer paid $8800 to a dance studio for lessons because he had been promised that the female instructors did far more than just dance. As it turned out, they didn't, and he claimed that he'd been robbed. The court was not sympathetic. Another taxpayer had a thoroughbred bird dog who just disappeared one day. The court, having seen a picture of the dog, admitted that it was a beautiful and very intelligent-looking dog and a prime target for dognappers. But just because he'd disappeared didn't mean that he'd been stolen.

Many theft losses are far from small. People have had maids who have cleaned them out on their last day of work.

Other taxpayers have been swindled royally. In 1973 hundreds of rich taxpayers discovered that an oil company in which they'd been investing millions of dollars was nothing but paper and mailboxes. What had looked like oil flowing through pipelines was actually orange paint.

Everybody suffers a casualty or theft loss now and then. Somebody stole a one-hundred-dollar plant in a sixty-dollar vase off my porch while I was writing this book. And the winter of '77 destroyed five trees in front of my house. The foliage loss may or may not be deductible, depending on how unusual the winter was for Washington, D.C. If this happened to our $23,000-a-year taxpayer, he could certainly add $60 in theft losses to the itemized deductions, for the plant and the vase, minus $100 nondeductible. We're up to $2010 in deductions. A tax savings of $562.80 at the 28 percent bracket. Still the zero bracket amount is worth more. So on we go.

Charitable Contributions

How much money do you give away every year? To your church, the American Cancer Society, the United Fund, the Red Cross? You can deduct these amounts—generally up to 50 percent of your adjusted gross income.

Can you imagine giving away 50 percent of your adjusted gross income? Before 1970 you could deduct only amounts up to 10 percent of your adjusted gross income. Apparently that wasn't enough for some people because Congress raised it to 50 percent. (For some contributions, the limit is 30 percent.)

Contributions to any U.S. organization operated "exclusively for religious, charitable, scientific, literary or educational purposes or for the prevention of cruelty to children or animals" are deductible. Your contributions to a charitable organization will be deductible only if the IRS has determined that the organization is in fact operated exclusively for one of the approved purposes. You're safe with the better-known charities, but watch out for those you've never heard of. Not only might your contribution serve no good purpose, but it may not be deductible either. Your local IRS office will tell you whether an organization has its approval.

Congress makes these contributions deductible because it wants these organizations to receive public support. That way Congress doesn't have to support them itself. Actually, Congress does support these organizations by giving them whatever it would have collected from the contributor as a tax. It's like a matching program. A taxpayer in the 50 percent bracket who gives $100 only *gives up* $50, since the other $50 would have gone to the government anyway. It's Congress who gives the other $50 by forgiving the taxpayer $50 in tax. The charitable-contribution deduction was started during World War I, when universities were pressed for funds. It was an instant success, and has been growing ever since, both in the amount deductible and in the kinds of organizations which qualify. Apparently without this deduction the support would not be there. Americans may be generous, but there are limits.

Let us say that you give away $100 every year—to your church or the Salvation Army or the March of Dimes. Add another $100 to the itemized deductions.

Now there are $2110 in itemized deductions. Still the zero bracket amount of $3200 is worth more in tax savings than the itemized deductions. Now you can begin to see why Congress doesn't make you go through all this, but lets you just reduce your adjusted gross income by $3200 (or $2200 if you are single).

But—if you own a house with a mortgage, the entire picture changes. As a rule, only indebted homeowners choose to itemize deductions.

Interest

When you buy a house with a mortgage, you pay a certain amount of money to the bank every month. Part of this sum is a repayment of principal—the money that you borrowed. The rest of it is interest on the money that you borrowed. The total monthly payment is always the same—but the parts which constitute interest payment and principal repayment change a little each month. This is because the bank wants you to pay most of the interest before you repay the principal. In the early years of the loan, the greater part of the monthly payments that you make is interest. Only a small part is repayment of principal. Under the Internal Revenue Code, the interest is deductible.

Virtually all interest that you pay is deductible. (We shall see one exception in Chapter 13.) The original reason for the deductibility of interest, even if it is paid in acquiring personal things, lies somewhere in congressional documents dating back to 1862. Some congressmen apparently thought that only business-related interest should be deductible. Others felt that all interest should be deductible, perhaps because the borrowing of money is always a businesslike matter. Congressmen from rural districts apparently feared that, if only business-related interest were deductible, their farmer-constituents would have trouble segregating interest on their farms from interest on their farmhouses. There were many rural districts back in 1862, and once the debate was over, all interest had become deductible, but the exact reason why is elusive.

Today, one reason may very well be that the government wants to encourage you to buy a house. After all, people who own houses are happy, stable people. They don't start riots or seek to overthrow the government. You will see that making interest deductible is a very effective incentive.

Suppose you have adjusted gross income of $23,000 and you have been renting an apartment for $425 per month.

That is a nice rental—under the 25 percent of your income which the economists say you should spend on housing. Now you decide to buy a house for $60,000. You pay $10,000 in cash and borrow $50,000 at 9 percent interest over thirty years. Your monthly mortgage payments will come to about $400. Besides that, you will have to pay utilities ($50 per month on the average), real estate taxes (let us say $80 per month), fire insurance ($20 per month), and repairs ($20 per month on the average). That comes to $570 per month. You can't afford it, right?

Wrong.

You have deductions. In the early years of the loan, nearly all the $400 of mortgage payments is interest—approximately $4800 per year, all deductible. Also, as a homeowner, you pay real estate taxes. On your $60,000 house, we have said that your real estate taxes amount to about $1000 which, like most taxes, is deductible. Deductions from your house come to $5800. Now remember, you had $2110 in deductions accumulated for other reasons (medical expenses, local income taxes, etc.). You wouldn't have used those other deductions without the house deductions. You would have taken the zero bracket amount of $3200. But with interest and taxes on your house, your itemized deductions amount to $7910, and the zero bracket amount—well, forget it! In fact, while on the subject of interest, don't overlook the car payments—good for another $50 per month of interest, or $600 per year. Plus another $20 per year in late payments on your credit card. Your deductions are up to $8530. That is a tax savings of $2224 per year, or $1328 more than the tax savings from the zero bracket amount. That $1328 per year breaks down to $110 per month. Your house doesn't cost $570 per month. It costs $460 per month because, without it, you would have been paying the government $110 per month more in taxes. Can you pay an extra $35 per month for a piece of property that is appreciating in value?

Here is the ironic part. If you were making $26,000 per year instead of $23,000, and had the same amount of deductions, the government would pay for even more of your house. At $26,000 the $8530 in deductions reduce your tax liability by $1440 more than the zero bracket amount does. The government pays for $120 of your monthly housing costs, and the cost is down to $450 per month.

The reasons for that are those tax brackets. Cast your eye over the percentage tax rates. At $23,000 all your income is taxed (at 1978 rates)

from $23,000 to $19,201, at 28 percent
from $19,200 to $15,201, at 25 percent
from $15,200 to $11,201, at 22 percent.

Your $8530 in deductions come off the top. They reduce your income to $14,470 and wipe out the tax in the 28 and 25 percent bracket and part of the tax in the 22 percent bracket.

At $26,000 your income is taxed

from $26,000 to $23,201, at 32 percent
from $23,200 to $19,201, at 28 percent
from $19,200 to $15,200 at 25 percent.

Your $8530 in deductions eliminate all the tax at 32 and 28 percent and part of it at 25 percent. When your income is higher, deductions eliminate income being taxed at higher rates.

In fact, if your salary is $32,000 per year, your $8530 in deductions give you a tax saving per year over the zero bracket amount of $1769. That is $147 per month. Your "rent" is down to $423 per month and you are making money by buying the house.

Is that fair? That the government pays for more of your house if you make more money?

The President doesn't think it is entirely fair. He proposes to limit the amount of the interest deduction to $10,000. You need a mortgage of more than $110,000 to run up $10,000 in interest each year (at 9 percent). So maybe the President doesn't think that it's unfair for the government to pay more for your house if you make more money. Only for the government to subsidize very expensive houses. Or maybe he figures that, as a practical matter, a limitation on the amount of deductible interest is the only politically feasible alternative. So far, the Congress has not gone along.

There are other deductions which can be counted if you itemize deductions. Mostly these are deductions for expenses you incur in a profit-seeking activity which, for one reason or another, are not deductible, as most business-type expenses are, from gross income. (You will soon see that the expenses of carrying on certain profit-seeking activities are deductible only if you itemize.) Since these deductions are business-like deductions, we'll get to them in the chapter on the business taxpayer.

Other deductions allowable when you itemize are some of those employee business expenses which are not deductible from gross income. We have already seen two of these—unreimbursed entertainment and education expenses. Some others include unreimbursed union dues, expenses for uniforms, or the cost of seeking a new job. Also, you may deduct expenses incurred "in connection with the determination, collection or refund of any tax"—tax counsel or assistance. Maybe the cost of this book is deductible.

You may be wondering whether there are any other personal deductions you can take. As we said earlier, there is a deduction for political contributions, but there is also a credit for political contributions, and we'll talk about it more in Chapter 9.

And that is it. There are no other personal, living-expense deductions. If you are wondering whether some other personal expense is deductible, forget it. Deductions are allowable under the Code only if the Code specifically provides for them.

You may have noticed, starting with your 1977 tax return, that you now reduce the total of your itemized deductions by $3200 if you file a joint return ($2200 if you are single). That is because of those new tax tables and rate schedules. They automatically reduce your income by $3200. So on your return you take $3200 off your itemized deductions—because your income is reduced by that amount automatically when you figure out your tax.

SEVEN
Exemption, Exemption, Who Gets the Exemption?

So now you have taken your adjusted gross income and reduced it one of two ways: automatically by the zero bracket amount, or by the total of your itemized deductions in excess of the zero bracket amount. You have come a long way, but you still don't know your taxable income. You have one more tax treat left: "people" deductions, also called "personal and dependent *exemptions.*"

You know all about the exemptions. One for you. One for your spouse. One for each child. Congress says that for every mouth you have to feed—even for your own mouth—you can knock another $750 off your income. (On your 1979 return the allowance per mouth will be $1000.) It's like a consolation prize. If you and your spouse have three children, Congress says, "You poor guy. Claim five exemptions and reduce your income by $3750." You do it, and then you have arrived at your taxable income.

The exemptions are just that simple for most people.

But for some people nothing is that simple. Maybe your younger child has his own income. What then? Or your older child has left home. Then what? Or your mother-in-law lives in the attic. Or your brother is a freeloader. Or . . . When things start to get complicated, the Code jumps right in and makes them worse.

Suppose your child does have income of his own. Can you still claim him as a dependent? Sure you can, as long as you provide more than half his support, and he is under nineteen. Even if he earns more money than you do. If he's a smart kid who banks it all and lets you support him, you can claim him as a dependent. Suppose he runs away from home and then earns more money than you do? As long as he banks it, receives more than half his support from you, and is under nineteen, he's your dependent. Your children (or stepchildren or children-in-law) under nineteen at the end of the taxable year are your dependents, wherever they live or whatever they earn, as long as you provide more than half their support.

Suppose your child is nineteen or over. He's still a dependent if he is a full-time student at a legitimate school during five months of the year. But if he is not a student, then he is *not* your dependent if he earns $750 or more during the year no matter how much support you provide. Before nineteen, he can earn more money than you do and still be your dependent. Once he turns nineteen, $750 exceeds the limit if he is not a student.

What about your mother-in-law living in the attic? She is your dependent too, as long as you provide more than half her support and she earns less than $750 per year. She doesn't even have to live in the attic. She can live across town, or across the country or halfway around the world, and still be a dependent. (But if she doesn't reside in the U.S. or Canada or Mexico, she must be a U.S. citizen.) She doesn't even have to be your mother-in-law. Most close relatives can be dependents: nieces and nephews, aunts and uncles, brothers and sisters and half-brothers and -sisters, and step-brothers and -sisters, and brothers- and sisters-in-law, parents and their ancestors, and stepparents and parents-in-law. Descendants of your children can also be your dependents, but not descendants of your stepchildren or children-in-law. Wherever they live. Whatever they do. As long as you provide more than half their support, and as long as they earn less than $750 per year. That magic number again. If they earn $750 or more, forget it. They're not your dependents. Your brother-in-law can live in your house, eat all your food, and run your air conditioners all day, but if he wins $750 at the racetrack, he's not your dependent.

People don't even have to be relatives to be claimed as dependents, but for nonrelatives there is one more condition: They must live in your house to be claimed as dependents. However, not all housemates can be dependents. Your mistress may live in your house, but she cannot be your dependent if your relationship with her is against the law where you live. Even if you support her and even if she earns less than $750. The government doesn't give you a tax break for living in sin.

Now, all that isn't really so complicated. The dependent rules are some of the most straightforward in the Code. But what if you are divorced and have kids? Then it's not so straightforward. Who's going to get those $750 exemptions? You? Your former spouse? Both? Neither?

The general rule is that a child of divorced parents is the dependent of the parent who has custody for the greater part of the year. You know the old saying: "Possession is 90 percent of the law." However, the parents can change this rule. If the mother has custody but the father provides at least $600 in support (or vice versa) and if the parents agree in writing (or if it is stipulated in a court decree) that the father can claim the child as a dependent, then Congress says, "We won't get involved in that," and it allows the exemption to the father. You can see that there is a need for tax planning even before getting divorced.

You can fight for that exemption if your former spouse won't agree to give it to you. If you provide more than $1200 per year for the child's support, and if your spouse cannot show that he or she provided more support than you did, then the exemption is yours. Both of you may have to submit itemized statements to the Internal Revenue Service. For divorced parents who still enjoy the fight, Congress provides the arena every April 15.

The question "what is support?" gets to be pretty important when you're counting up those dollars. Support includes things like lodging, clothing, medical and dental expenses, food, and education expenses. It also includes things like babysitting costs, movie money, Christmas presents, and recreation costs. The Tax Court has said that an expenditure is for support if it is for a "necessity." Not bare necessities, but things that are necessary for a healthy and reasonably happy child. "Reasonably" is the key. Money spent to spoil your child doesn't count toward support. One court said that expenditures for a speedboat and an expensive rifle could not be counted toward the support test. However, the money spent on an electric train did count. The IRS has said that the cost of a car can be counted; apparently a car is a necessity these days. (Be sure to register the car in your child's name if you want its cost to count toward support.) It's important to remember that money spent for something completely unrelated to support—such as paying the premiums on a child's life insurance policy—doesn't count.

When you are trying to determine whether you have paid more than half of someone's support, you do not have to compete with universities and foundations that give your children scholarships. While education expenses you pay count toward your share of support, scholarships are not counted in determining whether more than half the support has come from someone else.

Who is going to go through all this for one $750 exemption? For one exemption, probably no one. But if you have five kids, all living with your former spouse, and you are providing most of their support (in addition to supporting your paramour, for whom you can't claim an exemption), the exemptions are worth fighting for. After your spouse's divorce lawyer and the judge have picked you clean, you might as well try to salvage the dependent deductions.

People have been known to play fast and loose with exemptions. If they are married they have added a new exemption each year, for a biologically possible new baby who didn't happen to get born. These people are betting that no IRS agent will make you prove that you have children. Other people have been known to have children who capture the secret of perennial youth; they never seem to grow up and make a living. Thirty or forty years pass and the kid is still earning less than $750 per year and being supported by his family. The day of reckoning may not come for these people until the IRS realizes that you have more kids than is medically possible, or decides it's time for your child to strike out on his own. But this is tax evasion, not tax avoidance, and you must remember that a $750 exemption is only good for—at best—a tax savings of $525 and then only if you are in the 70 percent bracket. You must weigh the advantage of an extra $525 against the disadvantage of a ten-year jail sentence for tax fraud.

The President doesn't like the personal exemption. The way he sees it, it is designed to help you feed all those mouths, but since it is a deduction it is worth more to rich people and helps them feed mouths more than it helps poor people. The President would replace it with a tax credit of about $250. For every mouth you had to feed, you could reduce your taxes (as opposed to your income) by $250. That way, the exemption helps everybody equally. Even if this change were made, you would still have to decide whether you were feeding a particular mouth.

EIGHT
Tax Liability: Insidious Discrimination

Now you know the income on which you are going to pay tax, which Congress calls your "taxable income." You have added up all income (including everything specifically included, leaving out everything specifically excluded), and taken all your deductions—business deductions, personal deductions (standard or itemized), and "people" deductions or exemptions. The final figure is taxable income. You are ready to pay your taxes. You go to the tax charts, find your tax rate, and figure out how much you owe.

Tax charts. Plural. Not just one chart. Congress needed more than one chart to tell all the different kinds of taxpayers how much tax to pay. Four charts. There is one chart that shows the tax rates for "single taxpayers." It's called "Schedule X." There is another chart for "married taxpayers filing joint returns" and for "surviving spouses." It's called "Schedule Y." Schedule Y actually contains another chart for "married taxpayers filing separate returns." And then there is a fourth chart—"Schedule Z"—for creatures called "heads of households." Besides the charts, there is a form called "Form 4726," which provides a special method for rich people to figure out their tax; and there is a "Schedule G," offering a special method for all taxpayers.

Why are there four different charts with four different tax rates? Why do married people who file separate returns use a different chart from married people who file joint returns? Why do single people pay more taxes than married people? Why do rich people have their own special form? What is a "head of a household" and why is his tax different from both single people's taxes and married people's taxes? Why? Why? Why?

These questions and others could all be answered by reciting scores of legal principles. Instead, I'll tell you a story— a story rich in history and full of family feuds, with scheming, sex, and deception.

A Tale of Two Taxpayers

This is a tale of two taxpayers, and of their families and their government. These taxpayers didn't like to pay taxes very much, and neither did their families. Their government saw things differently.

The story starts in 1946. It was the best of times then because the war was over, and it was the worst of times because postwar taxes were high—even higher than today —and what could be worse than that?

What's Mine Is Mine; What's Yours Is Mine. Willie Washburn lived in Wyoming in 1946 with his wife Wanda. The Washburns lived right on the border of the state of Idaho— as close to Idaho as you could get and still be in Wyoming. The Washburns had a neighbor, Izzie Ireland, who was not married and who also lived close to the state of Idaho— closer than anyone, except for the Washburns.

In 1946 the Washburns had $20,000 in taxable income and they paid a tax that year of $6700. Izzie Ireland had the same taxable income, so he paid the same tax because there was no joint return in 1946, the tax rates were the same for everybody—married people, single people, or any other kind of people. Believe it or not, in 1946 there was only one tax chart and it was called "The Tax Chart."

In 1947 Izzie married a girl named Irene. And Izzie and Irene bought a lot just on the other side of the Washburns in Idaho. They built a house there, moved in, and became residents of the state of Idaho.

Willie Washburn said to Izzie: "Izzie, I think that is pretty dumb—to build a new house 50 yards away in the state of Idaho."

Izzie said: "Willie, I can save taxes by moving to Idaho."

Willie thought Izzie was pretty dumb to believe that too.

Well, it came to pass that in 1947 the Washburns had $20,000 in taxable income and they paid a tax of $6700. The Irelands had the same taxable income, but they paid a tax of only $4800. Now Willie thought that was *really* dumb since there still was only one tax chart, and he wrote to his congressman and asked why Izzie saved nearly $2000 in taxes just by moving to the state of Idaho.

A long time passed and then Willie's congressman responded.

Dear Willie:

    The reason why the Izzie Irelands pay less tax than you do is that the state of Idaho, where the Irelands live, is a "community property" state, while our beloved Wyoming is a "common law" state.

    In a community property state like Idaho, married people own all their property together. The home, the car, the bank account. Under Idaho law Izzie and Irene have equal property rights—50 percent each—in all their property. Even the family income. Izzie may be the only wage-earner in the Ireland home, but under Idaho law, Irene has a right to half his income.

    In "common law" states like our beloved Wyoming, married people do not automatically share their income equally. Each has a right to what is his. Since you are the only wage-earner in your family, you have a right to all the family income.

Under the federal tax laws, a taxpayer pays tax on whatever income he has a right to. Izzie and Irene each have a right to $10,000 of Izzie's income, and each files a tax return for $10,000. You have a right to all $20,000 of your income, so you file a tax return for that. Wanda, having no income, does not file a tax return.

Our great country's great tax system is a "progressive" tax system. The more income you have, the higher the rate of your tax. Izzie and Irene Ireland each pay tax on two smaller incomes at a lower rate. You pay tax on more income at a higher rate. That is why you pay more tax than the Irelands.

Rest assured that your congressman is doing all he can to remedy this injustice.

Sincerely,
Your Congressman

In fact, Congress was doing something. A number of states were community property states—California, Washington, and Oregon, to name a few besides Idaho, but most states were common law states like Wyoming. A difference in tax of $2000 went a long way in 1947, and some common law states were in the process of changing their laws to become community property states. Congress didn't think that a state should change all its property laws just because of the Internal Revenue Code.

What could Congress do? Two things. It could force the people in states like Idaho to pay taxes on what they earned, not on what Idaho law said they had a right to. Now that would have increased Izzie's taxes. Obviously Izzie's congressman would not vote for a bill like that. Or it could let people in states like Wyoming split their income for tax purposes just as people in community property states did, and get the same tax advantages. Willie's congressman, obviously, was more than happy to vote to decrease Willie's taxes. In 1948 the "joint return" was created.

By using the joint return, married taxpayers in all states

split their income for tax purposes just like people in community property states. Husbands and wives filed one return on their total income, but on the tax chart (used by all taxpayers back then), they looked up the tax on half of it, at a lower rate, and then doubled the result. Which was what Izzie and Irene had been doing in the first place by using two returns.

In 1948 Willie Washburn had $20,000 in taxable income. He and Wanda "elected" to file a joint return—something which any married taxpayers could do provided that they were married on the last day of the year. Willie found the tax on the tax chart for $10,000 of income, and doubled it. Low and behold: His tax was $4800.

Meanwhile, over in Idaho, Izzie and Irene could have each still filed separate returns for $10,000 of income, but with the new law, filing two returns just meant more paperwork with no tax savings. So the Irelands elected to file a joint return too, and they paid a tax of $4800. So the Washburns and the Irelands paid the same amount of tax. And Congress thought that the joint return was a pretty clever idea. End of Chapter One of my story.

Sex and the Single Taxpayer. In 1949 Willie and Wanda got divorced and Wanda moved away. Willie and the Irelands remained friends—at least until income tax time. Since Willie and Wanda were not married on December 31, 1949, Willie could not file a joint return. Instead he filed a single return and, with $20,000 in taxable income, discovered that he had to pay $6700 in taxes. Again, the Irelands, with the same taxable income, filed a joint return and paid a tax of $4800. Willie then wrote to his congressman to ask why, as a single taxpayer, he had to pay $2000 more in tax than Irene and Izzie Ireland.

Dear Willie:
    Last year you wrote to complain that the Irelands paid less tax

than you merely because they lived in Idaho. I had the Congress change the law so that married people everywhere paid tax at the same rate if they filed a joint return.

The most important thing about the joint return is that married people split their income and pay tax on two low incomes at low rates. Unfortunately, single people have no one to split their income with, and must pay tax on all their income at a higher rate. That is why, as a single person, you now pay more taxes than the Irelands. If it is any consolation, single people everywhere share your plight.

When we changed the law in 1948, we realized that single people would pay more taxes than married people. However, married people have greater living expenses than single people, and should therefore have to pay less tax than a single person on the same income. Also, married people are happier and contribute more to the national security.

Sincerely,
Your Congressman

And so, after 1948, all married taxpayers with the same income paid tax at the same rates, but single taxpayers with that income paid tax at a higher rate. Which was just too damn bad for single taxpayers, who were a threat to the national security in any event. (According to a 1948 poll, 50 percent of all communists were single.)

Help for Heads of Households. In 1950 Izzie and Irene Ireland had triplets, which proved to be too much for Izzie, who promptly dropped dead. When Irene filed her income tax return for 1950, showing $20,000 in taxable income, she discovered that she had to pay $6700 in taxes because Izzie had dropped dead before December 31, 1950, and she could not file a joint return. She promptly wrote to her congressman, complaining that, married or not, she still had three mouths to feed, besides her own, and why did she have to pay as much tax as Willie Washburn, who was living high on the heel, driving fast cars and bringing home slick women every night.

Irene's congressman agreed that the situation was despicable. In 1951 Congress passed a law which said that widows like Irene (or widowers) with children could continue to file a joint return for two years after their spouses died. Why two years? To give them time to adjust and maybe find a new spouse. Congress called people like Irene "surviving spouses."

Congress even went one better. It couldn't let Irene file a joint return forever because, with Izzie gone, Irene's living expenses were not as great. She didn't have to feed Izzie every night, or give him money to lose at the racetrack, or bowling money. On the other hand, it wasn't fair to make Irene pay as much tax as Willie Washburn, who was having such a good time. So Congress created a whole new tax rate for people like Irene whose two years as a surviving spouse were up but who still had children to feed: a rate that was higher than the rate for married people, but lower than the rate for single people. Not only could people who had been "surviving spouses" use this new rate, anybody who was unmarried but had dependents in the house could use it, even if they had never been married. Congress called these unmarried people with dependents "heads of households."

Now up until 1951 there was only one tax chart and everybody used the same chart (with married people figuring the tax on half their income and doubling it). Once Congress established altogether new rates for heads of households, it needed a new chart. So then there were two charts. It came to pass that the old chart, for single people, married people, and surviving spouses, was called "Schedule Y"; and the new chart, for heads of households, was called "Schedule Z."

The Single Taxpayer Is Saved but the Tax Avoider Is Trounced. Meanwhile, Willie and Wanda got back together and they had a son, Mort. So Willie no longer cared that single people paid much more tax than married people. But other people cared because in some instances single people were paying over 40 percent more in taxes than married people. For twenty years, single people fought for a reduction in their taxes. In 1969, with fewer voters getting married, Congress gave in. Starting in 1971, tax rates for single people were reduced so that they would never exceed the rate for married people with the same income by more than 20 percent.

With lower rates for single people, obviously married people and surviving spouses could no longer use the same tax chart as single people. Otherwise, married people would suddenly have lower rates, and that wasn't the point. So Congress gave single people a chart of their own. And it came to pass that this chart was called "Schedule X." And single people used the new chart, Schedule X, and married people and surviving spouses used the old chart, Schedule Y, and heads of households used Schedule Z. Also, since married people and surviving spouses now had Schedule Y all to themselves, there was no need to make them compute a tax on half their income and double it. So Congress revised Schedule Y and used rates which equaled twice the tax on half the income. After that, people who used Schedule Y just found the rate for their income and computed their tax.

By this time, Willie Washburn was a rich man. He was earning $60,000 each year in salary and had a portfolio in stocks and bonds which paid another $60,000 in interest and dividends. Willie was also becoming quite a dilettante in federal taxes. When he learned that Congress was planning to lower the tax rates for single people, he plotted a tax-avoidance scheme.

Willie figured that if he and Wanda filed a joint return showing $120,000 of income, they would pay a tax of nearly $60,000. However, Willie and Wanda weren't required to file a joint return. They "elected" to do that. If Willie gave his portfolio to Wanda, each would have income of $60,000. If each then filed a single return using the new, lower rates for single taxpayers, their tax would be $12,000 less.

Willie was so impressed with his tax scheme that he told everybody about it, including his congressman. His congressman was aghast at the idea of married people manipulating their income like that to lower their taxes, and he told his friends in Washington. The result was that, when Congress lowered the tax rates for single taxpayers, it raised the rates for married taxpayers who filed separate returns. If tax avoiders like Willie and Wanda chose to file separately, okay —but they would have to pay tax at the *old* rates for single people, which were higher. In fact, they were twice the rate for married people who filed joint returns. And Congress divided Schedule Y into two schedules—one with low rates for married people filing jointly, and one with high rates for married people who filed separately.

Relief for the Rich.   It is often said of Congress that the one hand giveth while the other taketh away. The reverse is also true. While Congress was snuffing out Willie's tax-avoidance scheme, it was giving him an altogether new tax break. Congress thought that the worst thing about Willie's tax picture was that part of his salary was being taxed at more than the 50 percent rate. With a salary of $60,000, Willie was paying a tax of 53 percent on all income over $52,000. Congress decided that there should be a maximum tax rate of 50 percent on income that a man earned by working. No man, it said, should have to work more than half of each day for the government.

In 1969, while reducing taxes for single people and stomping Willie's tax-avoidance scheme, Congress created the "maximum tax on *earned* income." Willie's portfolio income could still be taxed up to the 70 percent rate, because that wasn't earned income. But on money that Willie earned with the sweat of his brow, 50 percent was the tops. Since none of Congress's charts reflected the maximum tax rule, Congress created Form 4726—a special form used to figure tax by people with very high salaries.

The Marriage Tax. After all this activity over twenty years, you would think that the tax rates would be settled and fair to everyone. Not so. There still existed a disparity in the tax system, called the "marriage tax."

Willie Washburn's son, Mort, and one of Irene Ireland's triplets, Annie, grew up and became lovers. Mort had a job at which he earned $15,000 annually. Annie, being a modern woman, also had a job paying $15,000. Mort and Annie lived together. This disturbed Willie to no end, and he asked Mort why he and Annie didn't get married.

"Dad," Mort said, "as single taxpayers, Annie and I each pay about $2500 in tax, for a total of $5000. If we get married, we'll have to file a joint return showing $30,000 in income, and then we'll have to pay about $6000 in tax. We pay for our vacation each year with the $1000 in taxes we save by staying single."

Willie couldn't believe that. The joint return was supposed to lower married people's taxes. He dug out his tax books and, sure enough, he learned that once Congress lowered the tax rates for single people, a joint return reduced your taxes only if you and your wife were *splitting* income. If you were both working, and one was earning even half of what the other earned, you were piling income on top of income and paying taxes at a higher rate than if you stayed single. When Congress had created the joint return, almost all married taxpayers split the husband's income. The advent of the working woman changed all that.

The President, like Willie, does not approve of people living in sin and he has tried to do something about the marriage tax. At first he proposed to give people like Mort and Annie a deduction up to $600—a deduction of 10 percent of the first $6000 of income earned by the lower-paid spouse. That would have reduced Mort and Annie's taxes by about $240 if they got married. It would have helped but it would not have solved the problem entirely. As of this writing, the Treasury Department is still trying to develop a solution.

Willie couldn't wait for the Treasury Department. He came up with his own solution. Mort and Annie got married and, at Willie's suggestion, they now vacation each Christmas in Haiti, and they get divorced just before December 31. When they get home after the New Year, they get married again. That way, they are not married on December 31, and they must file single returns. The IRS is not pleased, and has announced that it will not recognize such divorces. In the end, the courts will have to decide.

That was how and why Schedules X, Y, and Z and Form 4726 came into being. First to treat married taxpayers the same in all states. Then to lower taxes for widows and other people with dependents, then to lower taxes for single people but prevent married people from taking advantage of the lower rates, and finally, to lower taxes for rich people. Someday there may be relief for married people where both spouses work.

You may have noticed on your tax return that, besides Schedules X, Y, and Z and Form 4726, there are the "tax tables" which can also be used to figure out your tax. The tax tables merely contain the results of doing the computations in Schedules X, Y, or Z for various amounts of income. Not everybody can use the tax tables, but people who can use them don't have to figure out their tax. The IRS has done it for them. In increments of $25 or $50, the IRS has figured the tax on all amounts of income up to $20,000 for single people and heads of households, and up to $40,000 for married people and surviving spouses. It's all there in the tax tables. You find the amount in the tax tables where your taxable income falls, read across, and find your tax. But the tax tables only go up to $20,-000 ($40,000 for married people). If your taxable income is greater, you must use the appropriate schedule, and compute your own tax.

Income Averaging

You may also have noticed on your tax return that there is another way to figure out your tax—"Schedule G." If you use Schedule G, you can forget about the tax you owe under Schedules X, Y, and Z. You can also forget about the tax tables and about Form 4726. You can forget about all of it.

Schedule G is the "income averaging" schedule. Not everybody can use Schedule G, but there are tax savings for those who can. Schedule G is not a schedule at all. It's a form on which you do up to twenty-one mathematical computations to figure out your tax. If your tax turns out to be less than the tax you owe under Schedules X, Y, or Z or the tax tables, then that is the tax you pay. Magic? No, "income averaging."

The income averaging rules are perhaps the most complicated rules in the Internal Revenue Code that apply to human beings (as opposed to corporate beings)—even worse than the medical-expense deductions. Here's what the Code says about income averaging (brace yourself):

Section 1301. Limitation on Tax. If an eligible individual has averagable income for the computation year, and if the amount of such income exceeds $3000, then the tax imposed by section 1 for the computation year which is attributable to averagable income shall be five times the increase in tax under such section which would result from adding 20 percent of such income to 120 percent of average base income.

Now what is that supposed to mean?

It means that if you have a lot more income this year than you have had in the past four years, you can reduce your taxes this year.

Let's go back to the medical-expense deduction pots and throw out all the medical bills. This time we have five pots and each pot represents a taxable year. Pot number 5 is the current year, say, 1978. Pot 4 is the previous year, 1977, and so on and down to Pot 1, which is 1974. Into Pot 1 we throw an amount of money which represents your taxable income in 1974. Let's say 1974 was a bad year and your taxable income was only $8000. Into Pot 1 goes $8000. Now comes Pot 2, 1975. Another bad year—maybe $9000 in taxable income. Pot 3, 1976, a slightly better year. Say $12,000. And Pot 4, 1977, better still, with $15,000 in taxable income. Now suppose in 1978 you hit it big—$30,000 in taxable income into Pot 5.

Congress looks at these pots and at what's in them and it says, "In 1978 you're going to be in the 36 percent bracket. But it's not really fair to tax you that heavily because, compared to 1978, you were broke from 1974 to 1977. So we will let you income-average."

What is income averaging? It is easier to understand what income averaging is if you understand *when* you can income-average.

You can income-average when the money in Pot 5 is much greater than the average amount of money in Pots 1–4. How much greater? Congress figures that if you are moderately successful, your taxable income will grow 20 percent anyway over the course of five years. No tax breaks for average growth. So you take the average of the amounts in Pots 1–4 and you take 20 percent of the average and add that to it. In our example, the average amount in Pots 1–4 is $11,000. Twenty percent of that is $2200. A total of $13,200 is the amount of taxable income Congress would expect you to have in 1978. For these calculations, that is called your "base income." Congress will give you a tax break only on 1978 income which is over and above that base-income figure. It calls that portion of your 1978 income "averageable income." (As a result of a highly technical transition rule, your base income for 1978 would actually be somewhat greater, but the principle of computing it is the same.)

Congress does not give tax breaks on just a little averageable income. Congress says your "averageable income" must be greater than $3000. In our example, $13,200 was the base-income figure. Income in 1978 is $30,000—$16,800 greater than base income; $16,800 is averageable income and it qualifies for a tax break. Restating the rule: Current income which exceeds 120 percent of your average income over the last four years qualifies for income averaging so long as the excess is greater than $3000.

What, again, is income averaging? Income averaging is a technique which lets you pay a tax on the "averageable income"—the excess—as though you earned it evenly over five years. Sometimes it is called a "five-year spreadback." Instead of paying a high rate of tax on all that averageable income in the current year, you figure out the tax on one-fifth of it (assuming you earned it on top of your base income), and then you multiply that tax times five. The procedure saves you tax because the first one-fifth of that averageable income will be taxed at a lower rate than the second fifth, and the third fifth, and so on. In short, you pay a tax five times on the first one-fifth of your averageable income, at lower rates, instead of once on all your averageable income at increasingly higher rates.

You also pay a tax on the base income—in our example, the first $13,200 of income. The total of the tax on the averageable income and the base income is your tax for the year.

In our example, the tax on $30,000 of current income under Schedule Y would be $6668. Under the income averaging rules, the tax would be $5960. Sometimes income averaging makes a big difference.

Why does Congress give you a tax break if your current income is much greater than in the past? Because under a progressive tax system you are supposed to be taxed in accordance with what you can afford to pay. In figuring out what you can afford to pay, it may be deceptive to look at just one year. Suppose in 1970 you had zero income. Then in 1971 you had $25,000 of income and paid a tax of nearly $4000. Is it fair to tax away about 15 percent of your income just one year after you were flat broke? Wouldn't it be fairer to say that during 1970 and 1971 you had an average income of $12,500 and that is what you should pay tax on? That is sort of what Congress is doing with the income averaging rules. Except that it looks at five years instead of two. Who knows—in 1969 you might have had $50,000 in income, and then you wouldn't need a tax break in 1971.

Not everybody can income-average even though the money in Pot 5 is much greater than the average money in Pots 1–4. As a general rule, income averaging is not available to people who have recently been in college or graduate school, unless they were supporting themselves during that time. Income averaging is designed mostly to help people like writers, who have high income in one year for work done in earlier years when they had little income. It can be used by anybody when the figures allow for it, but it cannot be used by people whooping it up in college, earning nothing and getting money from home every month, who then go out into the real world and land a high-paying job. Income averaging provides relief, not windfalls.

Income averaging is complex and you may want to seek help with it. But you should at least be aware of it so that you can inquire about it. You must elect to income-average. It is not something to which you are so firmly entitled that the IRS will advise you, if you fail to income-average, that it would be to your advantage to do so. If you overpaid your taxes because you used the wrong schedule, the IRS will alert you of this error, if its computers pick it up, because use of the proper schedule is due you. Not so for income averaging. Too many people overlook income averaging and pay more tax than they have to.

So now you know what your tax liability is. At least you think you do. In fact, you don't. After you have figured out your tax liability, you must reduce it by your tax credits, so that you don't pay too much tax.

NINE
Tax Credits

Of all the ways of reducing your taxes, tax credits are the best—the prize, the brass ring. If you owe $3000 in tax after all the figuring we've done so far, and are sitting there with a tax credit of $500 then you don't owe $3000. You owe $2500. Deductions are great—but they can't compare with tax credits. A $100 deduction means between $14 and $70 less in taxes, depending on your tax bracket. A $100 tax credit is $100 in your pocket.

Like most good things, tax credits are scarce and hard to come by. But most of them are not complicated. People often think that anything as beneficial as a tax credit must be highly sophisticated and very esoteric—only for the people with high-priced tax advisors. Not so. There are not many tax credits for individual taxpayers, but most of what is available is as simple as anything in the Code. Just assume that you are married, you have a child, hold two jobs yourself while your spouse looks for a job, you have a savings account and some stocks, and you give money to your favorite candidate. On those facts alone you are entitled to most of the tax credits in the Code.

The first tax credit is for the federal taxes that your employer withheld from your paychecks. Taxes you have paid during the year reduce the taxes you pay at the end of the year. Congress calls that a tax credit. Big deal.

The second tax credit is for the tax payments you made yourself during the year. These are the payments of estimated taxes you are supposed to make on income you receive which is not subject to withholding—such as interest, dividends, or royalties. Just like the first tax credit, you don't have to pay taxes twice. Pretty exciting.

The third tax credit is for your overpayment of Social Security taxes. Suppose your first employer paid you $19,000 for the year, and your second employer paid you $5000. The law says that both must withhold Social Security taxes from your paycheck. But the law also says that you only have to pay Social Security taxes on about the first $17,700 of 1978 income. Your first employer stopped withholding Social Security taxes at $17,700. But your second employer had to withhold on the $5000 he paid you anyway. So everything he withheld is an overpayment of Social Security taxes. You get a tax credit for that. Many taxpayers overlook this tax credit, and with the Social Security system in the condition it's in, the government doesn't exactly rush to point out their mistake. (In 1979, the wage base is scheduled to climb from $17,700 to $22,000.)

The fourth tax credit is for those political contributions you made. You get a tax credit equal to half the amount you contributed—but the largest credit you get is $50 if you and your spouse file a joint return ($25 if you are single). So if you made a political contribution of $100 or $150, you get a $50 tax credit. You reduce your tax liability by $50.

As an alternative, for 1978 you can take your political contributions as a deduction if you itemize. You can deduct up to $200 for political contributions if you file a joint return ($100 if you are single). But you can't have it both ways—a deduction and a credit. It's one or the other. Which do you want, the credit or the deduction? Figure it out. If you deduct it, a $200 contribution saves you $28 in tax if you are in the 14 percent bracket. It saves you $140 at the 70 percent bracket. If you take the credit, you save $50. It all depends on which bracket you are in. If you don't itemize deductions, then obviously you will take the credit.

Starting in 1979, the Congress has eliminated the deduction for political contributions. However, it has doubled the amount of the tax credit to $50 ($100 if you file a joint return). So all political contributors will get the same benefit. But for 1978, you can still take your choice.

The fifth tax credit you get is for "child care" expenses. Suppose your wife finds a job. Now you have to have a full-time babysitter for your child and a cleaning woman for your house. Today, that costs so much money that it may hardly be worth it for your wife to work. Congress, at the prodding of women's groups, decided to make it easier, financially, for your wife to work. It enacted the child-care tax credit.

You can take a tax credit for child-care or housecleaning costs. The credit is equal to 20 percent of the cost of employing a babysitter or cleaning woman. But if you have only one child, only the first $2000 of these expenses can be counted. So the maximum credit is $400. If you have two or more children, you can count the first $4000 of expenses. So the maximum credit in any event is $800.

Now your wife can't just horse around while she is supposedly working. She must have a legitimate job to get the full credit. Suppose you hire a live-in nanny who does everything for an annual salary of $5200. And then your wife gets a job for two hours each week and earns $500 per year. The rest of the time, with a nanny sitting at home, she drives around in her Mercedes and plays tennis. Can you get a tax credit of $400? No way. The child-care or housecleaning expenses that you count can never exceed the money your wife makes. So you get a credit of $100 (20 percent of $500).

Suppose your wife gets a better job than you've got. So you take the Mercedes and play tennis all day. That won't get you anywhere either. I have been talking in terms of "your wife" working just to keep it simple. But the limitation on the credit applies to whichever spouse earns less money. In this day of equality between the sexes, Congress doesn't care who stays home and takes care of the kids.

Child-care expenses—the expenses you count in figuring out the tax credit—include all amounts spent to employ a babysitter or housecleaner when you have children or other dependents under fifteen in your home.

They are called child-care expenses but they don't have to be spent on care for children. The credit is designed to help you or your spouse to work. If you have dependents fifteen or over living at your house who cannot care for themselves —such as an invalid mother-in-law—so that you need nurses or cleaning women if you and your spouse are to work, you can take the credit.

Babysitting expenses can be counted even if the services are performed outside your house—as in a day-care center. Nursing expenses for dependents fifteen or over must be for services performed in the house (there is no credit for nursing-home costs). Housecleaning expenses are counted only if the services are performed inside the house. If your maid won't do ironing and you have to take your shirts to the dry cleaners, there's no credit for that.

Until recently you could count amounts paid to relatives for child-care or household expenses only if your relatives were not claimed as your dependents and if you were supposed to pay Social Security taxes for them. You don't normally pay Social Security taxes for your parents, or your spouse's parents, and until recently there was usually no credit for amounts paid to them. Now Congress changed the law so that, starting with the taxable year 1979, you can count amounts paid to parents. As for your older children who baby-sit for the younger ones, payments to them cannot be counted if you are claiming them as dependents.

While the child-care credit was designed to help both spouses work, you can claim it even if you do not have a spouse, so long as you have dependents in your house who need to be watched or nursed.

For those who are energy conscious, Congress has provided another tax credit starting in 1978. This is popularly called the "home-insulation" credit. However, it is available not only if you install insulation in your home, but also if you do other work on your residence, work designed to reduce the amount of energy you use. The size of the credit: 15 percent of the amount spent on "energy-saving components" up to $2000, for a maximum credit of $300.

What are "energy-saving components"? Besides insulation, they are defined to include storm windows, storm doors, and a host of other materials and machines which reduce fuel consumption: replacement furnaces (or burners for furnaces) which are more energy efficient; an electrical or mechanical ignition system which replaces a pilot light on a furnace; automatic setback thermostats; caulking and weatherstripping; certain heat pumps; meters which display the cost of energy use; and anything else which the Treasury Department determines to be an energy-saver. It doesn't matter whether you own your home or rent it from someone else, as long as you try to cut your fuel bills.

Structural or decorative work does not count toward the credit. The cost of curtains, carpets, paneling, or exterior siding or even the replacement of a wall cannot be counted regardless of how much energy may be conserved. Also, using energy-saving equipment on a home you are building does not result in a credit. Congress expects you to do that anyway. It only encourages you to make changes in your present residence. For materials or equipment which can be counted, not only the cost of the merchandise but also the cost of labor for installing it may be used to determine the amount of the credit.

Timing is important to the availability of the credit. Energy-saving alterations made on or after April 20, 1977 and through December 31, 1985 qualify for the credit. If you installed insulation in the fall of 1977, you can claim a credit on your 1978 tax return. Note that the crucial date for purposes of claiming the credit is the date when installation is completed. If you installed insulation on April 19, 1977, but did not pay for it until April 21, 1977, there is no credit. On the other hand, if you paid for the job on April 19, 1977, but work was not over until April 20, the credit is available.

You do not have to claim the entire credit all at once. Up to $2000 of expenses made at any time during the qualifying period will result in a credit. Suppose you paid $700 in the fall of 1977 for insulation installed at the same time. You can claim a $105 tax credit on your 1978 return. Suppose also that in 1978 you put in storm windows at a cost of $500. That gives you an additional tax credit of $75. Total credit for 1978: $180.

Now suppose in 1979 you install a heat pump at a cost of $1000. A credit of $150 for 1979? No. You can count only the first $2000 of expenses for all energy-saving equipment. Since you have already counted $1200 for insulation and storm windows, only $800 of the cost of the heat pump can be counted—a $120 credit for 1979. And then you have used up your entire $300 credit. However, if you change residences, you can start all over again. The $2000 limit applies to each residence you own, through 1985.

Even greater tax credits are provided for the installation of solar, wind, or geothermal energy equipment—up to $2200 during the qualifying period.

What about the tuition tax credit? That tax credit that was

supposed to be available to people putting their children through college. It didn't quite make it through the 1978 Congress. The House passed a bill providing for a tuition tax credit. And the Senate passed a bill providing for a tuition tax credit. But the bills were different, and the House and Senate couldn't agree on what the tuition tax credit should be. Result—no tuition tax credit. The President was going to veto it anyway.

These are the credits for which many people qualify. They are not so difficult or mysterious or sophisticated. You don't need a tax lawyer to take advantage of them. There are other tax credits that are available for certain people in special circumstances. People who live in foreign countries, for example, can take a credit for part or all of the income taxes that they pay to the foreign country. That is called the "foreign tax credit." There is also a tax credit for people with very low incomes, and for elderly people with low incomes.

There is another tax credit for everybody, called the "general tax credit." You all know about the general tax credit: 2 percent of taxable income up to $180, or $35 per exemption. The general tax credit, which became effective in 1976, was Congress's way of making sure that during an election year you understood that it had reduced the income tax. If it had just lowered the tax rates, your take-home pay would probably have increased less than $4 per week and you might not have noticed it. Instead, at the end of the year you were permitted to cut your tax liability by up to *one hundred eighty dollars.* That you noticed.

Today, the general tax credit is built into the tax tables, like the zero bracket amount, so now you don't notice it unless your taxable income is greater than $40,000 (or $20,000 if you are single). But it is still there—at least for 1978. The general tax credit expires after 1978 (after an election year).

Another tax credit is the "investment tax credit," one of

the biggest. At the beginning of the book I said that tax credits were mostly for rich people and corporations. I was thinking of the investment tax credit, which is available only to people who invest. Rich people. People looking for tax shelters. So we'll talk about the investment tax credit in Chapter 13.

TEN
And for Those of You with a Little Something on the Side

In determining taxable income in the previous chapters, we reduced gross income by deductions available to everyone. Besides personal deductions, those deductions consisted of certain business deductions: transportation and travel expenses, moving expenses, and alimony. Back in the chapter on adjusted gross income, we saw that there were many business deductions for taxpayers who owned a business or carried on a trade, or were engaged in income-producing activities, but in that chapter we discussed only the ones available to employees. In this chapter, we will consider business deductions in general.

Among individuals, there are two kinds of business taxpayers. There are taxpayers who own a business or carry on a trade which is operated regularly; i.e., the person who owns a shoestore, a grocery, a bike shop; or a carpenter, a lawyer, a plumber, a writer.

There are also taxpayers who from time to time engage in activities which produce income but which may not rise to the level of a trade or business. These people do many things: They dabble in the stockmarket, buy and sell or rent real estate on occasion, build things in their workshop and sell them to their neighbors, or do other things to make money when the opportunity arises.

The Code says there is a difference between taxpayers who carry on a regular trade or business and taxpayers who merely engage in "income-producing activities." Code section 162 allows a deduction for the expenses of "carrying on a trade or business." Code section 212 allows a deduction for expenses "for the production or collection of income" and "for the management, conservation and maintenance of property held for the production of income." The reason for this distinction is mostly historical. Code section 162 has been around much longer than section 212. Before section 212 was enacted, one taxpayer tried to deduct under section 162 the expenses of dabbling in the stockmarket. The Supreme Court said that section 162 didn't allow such deductions since he was not "carrying on a trade or business." Congress responded by enacting section 212.

The rules on whether an expense is deductible are pretty much the same under both sections. But there is an important difference in how the expense is deducted. Expenses of carrying on a trade or business are deductible from gross income in determining adjusted gross income. Expenses incurred in income-producing activities are deductible from gross income in only one instance—if they are related to property which produces rents, like a house, or royalties, like a book. Otherwise, they can be deducted only if you itemize deductions. (Investments in partnerships are another matter which we will get to in Chapter 14.)

This difference in accounting for expenses from different activities becomes apparent when you examine a tax return. On Form 1040, you account for income and expenses from a "trade or business" on a separate form (Schedule C) and then you plug the result into the determination of gross income. If you have an overall profit from your trade or business, you add that to your gross income. If you have an overall loss, you reduce your gross income by the loss.

For income-producing activities, you use a separate form (Schedule E) and plug the results into the calculation of gross income—but only for rents or royalties. If you engage in some other income-producing activity—for example, you clip coupons or collect dividends from your stock—there is no special schedule for a separate balancing out of income and expenses from these activities. The income just gets added to gross income. The expenses are deductible (under "miscellaneous deductions") only if you itemize. If you don't itemize deductions and are making money with something besides rental property or property which generates royalties, you may have to include that income in your gross income without being able to deduct the expenses.

When is an activity a trade or business and when is it merely an income-producing activity? There are no set rules. If you have a store that you operate every day, clearly it is a business and your expenses are deductible from gross income under section 162. If you play the stockmarket in your spare time, that clearly is not a trade or business, and your expenses, such as your subscription to the *Wall Street Journal* or your postage or telephone costs, are deductible only if you itemize deductions. If you do carpentry work regularly on the weekends, or sell cosmetics to the neighbors, you are probably carrying on a trade or business. But if you just work in your workshop and sell a bench that a neighbor saw and liked, the expenses of building it are deductible only if you itemize deductions. If you own property that produces rents or royalties, expenses are deductible from gross income no matter how infrequent the activity.

Are You Out to Make Money?
Or Are You Just
Having a Good Time?

In order to take all the business deductions in the first place, you must be seeking to make a profit. Remember, Congress gives you these deductions so that you will go into business and make money which it can tax. If you are not out to make money, Congress is not interested in giving you many deductions. If you have a hobby which generates a little income but mostly costs you money, Congress does not let you call that a business and use all those losses to offset income from other sources. If you are just out to have a good time, you cannot deduct the full cost of that.

Consider the man who owns a farm where he goes to relax on the weekends. He raises two milk cows and grows three ears of corn each year, for an income of $200. He claims he's in the farming business, and he tries to deduct the $250 in fire insurance premiums on his barn and the $1000 in salary he pays to the caretaker. (For reasons which will become apparent later on, we will assume that these expenses are related only to his barn or fields, not to his farmhouse.) Congress doesn't allow him to deduct all those expenses. He can deduct the interest and taxes and casualty losses on the barn (or even on the farmhouse) because everybody can deduct these expenses as long as they itemize deductions, but the cost of insurance on the barn and a caretaker for the cows and the corn are personal expenses which usually are not deductible. To deduct all those expenses, he must show that his farm was really a business and that he was out to make a profit.

When are you out to make a profit? Obviously, if you make a profit you have a profit motive (Congress doesn't really care what your motive is when you're churning out that taxable income). It gets difficult only when you don't make a profit. Then the IRS wants to know why you are doing what you do. Are you really trying to make money on that farm, or are you just horsing around and trying to deduct all the expenses of your weekend hobby? Do you honestly hope to make a profit selling birdhouses, or do you just work in your workshop because it beats mowing the lawn? The test of profit motivation is an objective one. The IRS says that the determination of whether an activity is engaged in for profit depends on a number of factors. For example, how is the activity carried on? In a businesslike manner, or like a circus? How much do you know about what you're doing? How much time do you spend doing it and is it a recreational or pleasurable activity that you would spend time on anyway? How much other income have you got? Have you made money doing this in the past? The IRS tosses these and other questions around. No one question is determinative. The IRS listens to your story and makes up its mind. If it decides that you're out to make money, you can deduct all the expenses. If it decides your so-called business activity is a hobby or recreation, your deductions will be severely limited. If you don't like the IRS decision, you can take it to court and try again.

Some people are not too enthusiastic about this objective test. They feel they need time to show that their farm can turn a profit, or to make their birdhouses a commercial success. For these people, there is another test. The "two-out-of-five test."

Under the two-out-of-five test, there is a *presumption* that you have a profit motive if in fact you have made a profit during two of the last five years (including the current year). If your income from the activity exceeds all your deductions from the activity in any two of five years, you are presumed to have a profit motive, so you can deduct all expenses for all years. The IRS can still try to overcome the presumption, but as a practical matter no questions are asked if you pass the two-out-of-five test. (If you are in the horse business— breeding, training, racing, or showing—you only have to show a profit in two out of seven years. There are two reasons for the longer test for horse people. One, it's hard to make money in the horse business. Second, horse breeders have effective lobbyists in Washington.)

If you don't make a profit in two of five (or seven) years, that doesn't necessarily mean that you don't have a profit motive. All it means is that you lose the presumption that you do. You can still try to show a profit motive under the objective test.

Question: If you lose money in the first year you engage in your so-called business activity, how do you know whether you can deduct all your expenses? Answer: You don't know. But if you want to, you can elect to have the two-out-of-five rule apply, and then you can go ahead and deduct all the expenses in year one. Here's how that works. You buy your farm in year one, make $200, and pay the caretaker $1000. You add the $200 to your income and deduct $1000 as a business expense. The IRS comes along and says, "We don't think you intend to make any money on this farm. We think raising cows and corn is just a weekend hobby." You say, "I elect the two-out-of-five rule." Then the IRS backs off and lets you deduct all $1000 in the first year. It also lets you deduct all $1000 in the second year, and in the third year. But if you haven't made a profit after the fourth year, you are in big, *big* trouble. Because the IRS is then going to send you a tax bill for years one, two, and three, when you deducted all those expenses you shouldn't have deducted.

Suppose the IRS doesn't notice your deduction in the first year? Then you just keep your fingers crossed. It may never notice. But if it catches up to you in your second year, and you decide to elect two-out-of-five, the election relates back to the first year. You don't have four more years to try to turn a profit; once you elect, you look at five-year periods starting with the first year. If the IRS doesn't catch up with you until the fifth year, you better have made a profit in two of the years if you want to elect two-out-of-five.

If you do turn a profit in two of the first five years, you don't necessarily have a license to lose money. The IRS may come after you again during the next five years and you may have to elect once more.

The two-out-of-five election is a little risky. If you don't make a profit during two years, you will owe back taxes (with penalties and interest). In fact, you may have to sell the farm to pay the taxes. This is why some people prefer to slug it out up front over the objective test.

Can you elect the two-out-of-five test after you have lost the battle over the objective test? As a practical matter, you probably cannot. The two-out-of-five test must always be elected within sixty days after the IRS has notified you that it intends to disallow your so-called business deductions. You may not have time in sixty days to slug out the objective test. The whole purpose of the two-out-of-five test is to reduce the time the IRS spends fighting with you over the objective test, and to weed out the people who don't really expect to make a profit even over five years.

What happens if it is determined that you do not have a profit motive? Well, if you don't have a profit motive, then this so-called business of yours reveals its true colors. It's just a hobby. A pastime. A personal thing. And personal expenses are not deductible unless the Code specifically says so. Back to our weekend farmer. He pays the caretaker of his farm $1000. Assume also that he pays a real-estate tax on the barn of $100. If he fails the profit motive test—if his farming operation is a hobby—well, the Code specifically allows a deduction for real-estate taxes, even if they relate to hobbies, so he can deduct the $100 he pays in real-estate taxes. But there is no specific deduction for a salary you pay to someone to look after your hobby. Expenses like that may be deducted only if you have a profit motive. So the caretaker's salary is not deductible.

Now our weekend farmer might say, "Hold everything. I have $200 in income from my farm—from selling the corn and the milk. Obviously I must pay taxes on that income. So why can't I deduct the salary I pay the caretaker?"

He has a legitimate gripe. The fact is, if he can show that the caretaker took care of the cows and watered the corn, he can offset his income from the farm by the caretaker's salary—but *only* his income from the farm. And before he can deduct the caretaker's salary from farm income, he must reduce farm income by the deductions from the farm which he can take anyway, such as the real-estate taxes. To calculate how much of the caretaker's salary (or the cost of fire insurance or repairs to the barn) he can deduct, our weekend farmer reduces his $200 in farm income by the $100 in real-estate taxes which he can *always* deduct. That leaves him with $100 in farm income against which hobby expenses can be offset. On his tax return he can reduce that $100 of remaining farm income to zero—but not below zero—by deducting $100 of the salary he paid to the caretaker. The rest of the caretaker's salary is not deductible. And remember, to be able to deduct even $100 of the caretaker's salary, he must show that $100 worth of the caretaker's time was devoted to the cows and the corn.

When you have income from a hobby which does not meet the profit-motive test, you can deduct hobby expenses only to the extent necessary to reduce that income to zero, and then only after it has been reduced by related expenses which are always deductible. (If our weekend farmer had also paid $500 in interest on a mortgage on his barn, he could have deducted that too, but then his "always deductible" expenses—interest and taxes—would have wiped out his farm income altogether, so none of the caretaker's salary would be deductible.) That is the consequence of not having a profit motive. Congress doesn't tax your hobby income if you have expenses to offset it. But it also doesn't let you use your hobby expenses to offset other income, such as your salary.

So You Are Out to Make Money

If you do have a profit motive, then the question becomes, What expenses can you deduct? The Code says that you can deduct *all* expenses related to your business activity. But that is not the whole story. There are a number of limitations on business-expense deductions. The most important limitation is that the expense be an "ordinary and necessary" one, a rule we referred to in Chapter 5, and we will talk about that limitation first. There are other limitations: Some expenses cannot be deducted because it would be against "public policy" to allow their deduction; for other expenses, allowing their deduction would make it too easy to avoid paying taxes at all. We'll get to these limitations later. We will also get to other business deductions, such as "depreciation," and to the "investment tax credit."

Obviously an expense has to be "necessary" for your business activities in order to be deductible. Suppose the rental property which you own has a leaky roof, and just as you are preparing to fix it, you learn that the American Roofers Association is holding its annual convention in Antigua. You and your spouse decide to attend the convention to learn something about fixing roofs and to meet some roofers. Clearly you cannot deduct the cost of the trip to Antigua as a business expense. It is not "necessary" to go to Antigua to get the roof on your rental property repaired.

Assuming that the expense is a necessary one, then you must decide whether it is an "ordinary" expense. The reason you must decide whether it is "ordinary" is that only "ordinary" expenses are deductible currently—that is, in the year in which they are incurred. If an expense is not an ordinary expense (but is still a necessary one) then it is called a "capital expenditure," or a "capital item," and you can only deduct it over a period of years. You are then said to "capitalize" your expense. (Capital expenditures have nothing to do with the capital gains.)

Most taxpayers prefer to deduct business expenses currently because they paid them currently (or at least became obligated to pay them), and because they almost always want to reduce their taxes in the current year. They will worry about next year next year. Consequently taxpayers spend a lot of time and money arguing with the Internal Revenue Service over what is meant by an "ordinary" expense.

Suppose after you return from Antigua, you get the leak in the roof of your rental property repaired. The cost of the repair is an "ordinary" expense (and a necessary one) and you can deduct it currently. Suppose, however, that by the time you return from Antigua, the roof has become a sieve, and instead of patching it up you get a whole new roof. That is a capital expenditure, and you must deduct the cost of the new roof over a period of years, or "capitalize" it. How many years? The number of years in the expected life of the roof. Say the roof is expected to last ten years. You divide the cost by ten and deduct one-tenth each year. (In capitalizing costs, you must also account for something called "salvage value," which we shall deal with later on.)

If you spent $300 patching up the roof, you could deduct all $300 currently. If you spent $2000 putting on a new roof that is expected to last ten years, you could deduct only $200 currently. Next year, you would deduct another $200, and so on for ten years. You can see that the question of whether the expense is "ordinary" or "capital" is important to your business activities.

As with many important questions in the tax law, the question of whether an expense is "ordinary" depends on the facts in each case. Consequently there are no rules of law that always give you the right answer. Courts have attempted to develop principles which help resolve the question, but often the principle turns out to be limited to the facts of the case in which it was developed.

"Ordinary" expenses have been described as "normal or customary," and this is probably the safest explanation. Normal or customary expenses often are recurring expenses, such as rent, advertising, or postage, but they don't have to be. They might be paid only once by a taxpayer but they are still "ordinary" because they are the kind of expense which other taxpayers in the same situation would be expected to make. For example, if you were sued in a matter involving your business activities, and incurred heavy legal fees, the fees would be deductible currently, even though you might never be sued again. Defending your business activity is a normal and customary thing to do.

"Ordinary" expenses are often expenses which are used to acquire something tangible or intangible which serves your business for no more than one year. For example, if you are an investor, your subscription to the *Wall Street Journal* is deductible currently, since last year's *Wall Street Journal* doesn't do you much good. But if you purchased a set of investment reference books that could be good for five years, you'd probably have to capitalize them.

Not surprisingly, the IRS often views ordinary expenses as small expenses, while capital expenditures are large expenses.

The IRS has issued rules on distinguishing between "ordinary" expenses and "capital" expenditures for one business deduction—repairs to business property. We have already seen that patching the roof is ordinary; replacing it is capital. The IRS says that "the cost of incidental repairs which neither materially add to the value of the property nor appreciably prolong its life, but keep it in an ordinarily efficient operating condition [the repairs to the roof], may be deducted as an expense." However, "repairs in the nature of replacements, to the extent that they arrest deterioration and appreciably prolong the life of the property" [the new roof] shall be capitalized. In the house you rent out, the cost of painting it every year is an expense which can be deducted currently because that doesn't "materially add to its value" or "appreciably prolong its life." Wallpapering the inside would be treated the same way, as would sanding the floors. Repairing the sink would be an expense. But remodeling the entire bathroom would be a capital expenditure. Note that the bathroom might be nonfunctional, and you might argue that remodeling it was a "repair," but since remodeling would "materially add to the value of the property" and "arrest deterioration and prolong the property's life," it wouldn't be treated as a repair.

These IRS rules are intended to govern repairs, but the Service sometimes applies them to other expenses too, allowing a deduction only if the expense accomplishes something, or acquires something, that lasts less than one year. But this test doesn't always work either. A new carburetor installed in your business car might last more than a year, and yet the cost of it is clearly an ordinary expense because it does not "appreciably prolong" the car's life nor "materially add" to its value.

Maybe the rule for distinguishing between ordinary expenses and capital expenditures should not be couched in legal terms. Instead, consider your business activity as nothing more than taking care of one matter after another. Look at your expenditure in terms of the matter it takes care of. If you know that the matter will be back before too long, it is probably an ordinary expense. If you feel you won't have to bother with that for a while, it was a capital expenditure. You're incurring expenses if you are just keeping things in shape. You're making capital expenditures if you are improving them.

Watch Out for "Public Policy"

Some business expenses cannot be deducted even though they may be ordinary and necessary. Some taxpayers will do anything to make a dollar, and Congress has decided that, as a matter of public policy, it should not allow a deduction for the expenses of certain undesirable activities. Bribes and kickbacks, for example, cannot be deducted. To some people, bribes and kickbacks may seem a necessary expense, and in some businesses it may be perfectly normal and customary. Still they are not usually deductible.

A bribe or a kickback made to any federal official may never be deducted as a trade or business expense. Even if it's not made to an official but is illegal under federal law, it's not deductible: It's against the "public policy." A bribe or a kickback made to a state official is also against public policy and not deductible. However, a bribe or kickback to a nonofficial, even though it is illegal under state law, *is* deductible so long as the law is not generally enforced. If you want to deduct bribes or kickbacks, make them to nonofficials in a state where everybody does it.

Also nondeductible as a business expense are fines or penalties for violations of laws. If you are caught speeding to a meeting with a client, you cannot deduct the speeding fine. If you get a parking ticket because you were late for the meeting anyway (having been stopped for speeding) and double parked, you cannot deduct the parking fine. If you tried to bribe the policeman who gave you the speeding ticket and were fined for bribing a police officer, you cannot deduct that. (And, of course, even if you successfully bribed him, you cannot deduct that either.)

Expenses which are not deductible because they are bribes or kickbacks, or fines or penalties, should not be confused with expenses incurred in illegal businesses. Expenses incurred in illegal businesses are normally fully deductible. The Supreme Court once allowed deductions for the expenses of running an illegal gambling operation. Rent, employees' salaries, supplies—it was all deductible even though the business was illegal. Of course, the gambling income had to be reported. As I said in Chapter 1, for tax purposes the government doesn't care where you get it as long as you pay taxes on it.

Writing Off Your Home

Some business deductions which used to be taken regularly are now severely limited. Two of these deductions were favorites among taxpayers: the "vacation-home" deduction and the "home-office" deduction.

Ordinarily the expenses of maintaining a home—repairs, insurance, telephone bills, utility bills—are not deductible; they are personal living expenses. (Interest, taxes, and casualty losses are, of course, always deductible.) Back in the good old days, some taxpayers would deduct part of their home maintenance expenses anyway. They would put their house to income-producing use. If they had a house at the beach which they used one month each year, they would try to rent it the other eleven months. Then regardless of how long they rented it or whether they rented it at all, they would claim that the house was income-producing property, and they would deduct all maintenance costs for eleven months. Sometimes the IRS would challenge these deductions under the profit-motive test. Sometimes it would win but often it would lose.

Or if a taxpayer had a desk and a pencil in his home, he would say that part of his house was an office used to generate part of his salary, and he would try to deduct part of the expenses of maintaining his home. Now how did the IRS know if he did office work at his desk or just did the Sunday crossword puzzle? This taxpayer often ended up in court too.

Naturally no two judges in the country could agree on when any of these deductions were proper. In 1976 Congress decided to set down some "clear-cut guidelines" for vacation-home and home-office deductions. You may recall how much success Congress had with its clear-cut guidelines on scholarships and fellowship grants. It remains to be seen whether Congress does any better this time. The guidelines are tough on taxpayers, and when taxpayers get cornered they can usually fog up anything which is remotely clear-cut.

The Vacation-Home Deduction. Taxpayers with a little cash who grew tired of paying $100 every weekend to a beach hotel, or $700 each week for a beach cottage, came to realize that if they bought a beach house, other renters would pay for half of it and the government would pay for much of the rest. Their vacations at the beach were almost free.

Suppose a taxpayer bought a house at the beach for $60,-000, paying $10,000 in cash. We have already seen that the before-tax cost of a house like that is about $7000 annually. If he rented out his house during the year for a total of $5600, the cost would be down to $1400. He also had about $6000 per year in deductions for interest and real-estate taxes, but those deductions were used mostly to eliminate the $5600 in rental income that he had. So while those deductions kept him from having to pay any tax on the rental income, they didn't reduce his taxes on other income very much—maybe by $200. The house still cost him $1200 per year.

But that wasn't the whole story. The vacation-home-owner could reduce the cost of his house even more, thanks to the government. Since the house was "income-producing property," he could take other deductions besides the interest and taxes. He could deduct a portion of the expenses of owning the property—such as repairs and insurance—the portion allocable to the time the property was used to produce income. These were expenses he could not deduct for the house which he only lived in. He would probably even deduct the expense of a trip to the beach to "inspect" the property. Now these expenses wouldn't amount to much, maybe another $1000 per year in deductions, which saved him another $300 a year in taxes and reduced the cost of his house to $900. But there was another deduction that he could take. There was the "depreciation" deduction. To fully understand the tax benefits of a vacation-home (or a home-office), you must understand depreciation.

Depreciation is a deduction that you get because you have property which decreases in value. The strange thing about depreciation, though, is that your property doesn't really have to decrease in value. It just has to decrease in value for purposes of the tax laws. And under the tax laws, *everything* decreases in value. Even if it increases in value.

If you bought a house for $60,000 and sold it the next year, somebody would probably pay you up to $66,000 for it. That is what it would be worth. If you sold it after two years, someone might pay you up to $72,600 for it. In real life, residential property often increases in value at rates as high as 10 percent per year (even higher in some locations).

But not in the fantasy world of the tax laws. Property *decreases* in value under the tax laws. After all, property gets old. It gets older every year. In a house, the plaster starts to crack, the roof leaks, and the wood rots around the windows. The property just wastes away. It may well be worth more every year in dollars, but it is wasting away just the same. Under the tax law, you get a deduction for that wasting away. It's called the depreciation deduction.

You can take a depreciation deduction for all business property except land. Houses, buildings, automobiles, machines, airplanes—all business property except land is depreciable. The fact is, a great deal of business property does decrease in value because a great deal of business property is machinery. But some business property is real estate, and in the real world that rarely decreases in value; nonetheless, the Code says it decreases in value. So you get a depreciation deduction for it anyway. Don't fight it. Just take advantage of it while it lasts. (We will look at other rationalizations for depreciation in Chapter 13.)

What is the amount of the depreciation deduction? It is the amount by which your property is said to decrease in value each year. The kind of property which individuals own is often said to decrease in value evenly—that is, by the same amount each year for a number of years. The amount depends on your "basis" in the property—which is usually what you paid for it—and on how long you can expect it to be useful. If you paid $1000 for it and you expect to be able to use it for ten years and then throw it away, it decreases in value $100 each year. That is your yearly depreciation deduction. If, after ten years, the property is expected to have a value of $100, then it is said to have a "salvage value." In computing depreciation you are supposed to subtract salvage value from your cost, and then divide by the number of years of useful life. However, for personal property with a useful life of three years or more, salvage value can be disregarded if it is expected to be 10 percent or less of the property's cost or "basis" (more on "basis" later).

When, under the tax laws, property is said to decrease in value evenly over its useful life, we call that "straight-line depreciation." If you plotted the decrease in value of your property on a graph, the value would fall in a straight line. Sometimes property is said to decrease in value even faster —and we call that "accelerated depreciation"—but we won't worry about that now.

How do you know how long you expect your property to be useful? One way is through experience. If you buy cars for your business, you may figure that usually your cars will be economically useful for about three years. After that, repairs will cost so much that you would do better to buy new cars. Your typewriters may last five years. So long as your estimate of useful life is reasonable—something close to what other people in the same business would estimate— you can go on your own experience. If you are not sure how long your property will be useful, or if you don't want to risk the IRS disagreeing with your estimate, the IRS will tell you how long it should be useful. It has compiled data on the expected useful life of different kinds of properties and you can use its figures and then you are safe.

Any property which you use in a business or to produce income, except land, can be depreciated. Now go back to the beach house. It is property held for the production of income. So it is depreciable.

The useful life of a frame house is usually figured at around thirty years. Everyone knows that there are two-hundred-year-old frame houses around, but no matter. Most people agree that you can hold a frame house economically for thirty years. (A house can never have a shorter useful life than the term of the mortgage.)

You paid $60,000 for the house but $10,000 of that was attributable to the cost of the land. So the cost of the house was $50,000. Now, you use this house yourself one month each year. So only eleven-twelfths of the cost of the house was for property used for the production of income. The cost of your house for purposes of depreciation, therefore, is about $45,000. After thirty years, you figured, the house would have a salvage value of $5000 (which would be eleven-twelfths of the entire salvage value). So your yearly depreciation was $1333 ($40,000 divided by 30). You got a deduction each year of $1333. That saved you another $400 in tax. The cost of your house, after depreciation, insurance, and repairs was down to $500 per year, thanks to the U.S. tax laws.

The IRS didn't always let you get away with that. It would ask, "Do you really have a profit motive? Or is pleasure your primary reason for owning that house?" A strong point for the IRS was that rents on vacation property seldom exceeded costs. On a cash-flow basis, vacation-homes lost money (and they were often used by the owners during the highest-rent season). A strong point for taxpayers was that vacation-homes increased in value. If they sold the place after a few years, their profit would wipe out any cash-flow losses. Doubtlessly, the IRS lost a case for each case it won.

In 1976, when Congress was in a tax-reforming mood, it decided to put a stop to the litigation. It wrote new rules limiting deductions for vacation homes or other "dwelling units" which you both rent out and use for your own purposes. "Dwelling units" includes house-trailers and houseboats.

You are subject to the new rules if you use your vacation home yourself more than fourteen days during the year. At first this fourteen-day rule was going to be the only limitation. Then Congress decided that if you rented your vacation-home most of the year, you should be able to use it more than fourteen days and still avoid the new rules. So it added an alternative limitation: You can use your vacation-home up to 10 percent of the number of days it is rented (if that turns out to be more than fourteen days of personal use) and still avoid the new rules. So if you rent your vacation-home two hundred days per year, you can use it yourself twenty days. The only people who can use their vacation-home for a month, and still avoid the new rules, are people who rent their homes at least three hundred days per year.

What are the new rules? What happens if you use your vacation-home more than fourteen days or more than 10 percent of the time you rent it? The new rules say that you are automatically treated as if you do not have a profit motive. You fail the profit-motive test, period.

What happens when you fail the profit-motive test? As with your farm, your deductions cannot exceed the amount of rental income which is left over after you have reduced rental income by the "always deductible" expenses, such as interest or taxes. But the rules are a little different from the farm.

With the farm, you reduced income from the farm by the *total* amount of your "always deductible" expenses. If you had net income from the farm left over, on your tax return you reduced that net income to zero by the expenses which are deductible only if you have a profit motive, such as the caretaker's salary.

For your vacation-home, you don't reduce rental income by the *total* of your "always deductible" expenses in order to determine how much of those other expenses are deductible. You reduce rental income only by a portion of those "always deductible" expenses—the portion which is allocable to the period of time the property was used as rental property. You allocate the "always-deductible" expenses between personal use and business use.

Suppose you rent your beach house sixty days each year and live in it yourself thirty days each year (the other nine months the house is not used at all, for business or pleasure). The house is therefore used two-thirds of the time as business property. Now suppose that interest payments on the house for the year amount to $4800. You don't reduce your income from the house by $4800 (as you did with the farm) to determine how much of the other expenses may be deductible. You reduce rental income by two-thirds of $4800, or $3200, because only two-thirds of that interest was for property used as rental property. (The remaining interest is claimed as an itemized deduction.)

Once you have reduced rental income by the portion of the "always-deductible" expenses allocable to the property's use as rental property, then on your return you can offset this "net rental income" (if any) by the expenses which are deductible only if the property is business property, such as maintenance, fire insurance, repairs, and depreciation. But remember that these expenses must also be allocated between business and personal use. For example, if you paid $300 for fire insurance, you could deduct only $200 from net rental income—because one-third of that fire insurance covered the house while it was being used for personal reasons. The same would be true for repairs. And you could depreciate only two-thirds of the cost of the house.

Why must the income from the farm be reduced by the

total of your "always-deductible" expenses while the vacation-home income must be reduced only by the portion of
always-deductible expenses allocable to its use as rental
property? The Congress does not really tell us. Note that the
vacation-home rule is better for you because it leaves more
rental income which can be offset by maintenance and similar expenses and by depreciation (and the "always deductible" expenses can always be claimed as itemized deductions). When the new rules were under consideration, some
congressmen wanted to treat vacation-homes like hobbies—
like a farm. More conservative congressmen felt that owning a vacation-home could be as much a profit-oriented investment as it was a pleasurable activity. After all, some
vacation-home owners are serious about generating income
to pay for their homes, unlike our weekend farmer. A com-
promise was finally struck with the rules described above.

Suppose you use the house yourself fourteen days or less,
or only 10 percent (or less) of the time that it is rented? Then
you are not subject to the new rules. You don't fail the
profit-motive test automatically. If you can show a profit
motive, you can deduct repairs, insurance, and depreciation
allocable to the business use of the property even if these
expenses and the always-deductible expenses exceed rental
income.

Observe that the new vacation-home rules have not eliminated all the tax benefits of owning a vacation-home. The
interest and taxes on the house are always deductible and
may prevent any tax on rental income. If they exceed rental
income, they will still offset other income and reduce your
taxes. To that extent the government still helps you pay for
the house. You just can't use depreciation or maintenance
expenses to offset your other income.

Observe also that, if you want to vacation at the beach for
a month, the new rules are easily avoided if you buy two
houses. You use each for two weeks. The rules are also
avoided if you own a winterized house which you rent for

eleven months. Then you can use your house more than thirty days each year. Which means that rich people who can afford two houses or a year-round vacation house may not be affected at all by the new rules. It was these people whom Congress was supposedly gunning for in the first place. It just happened to miss.

These vacation-home rules are also applicable in the case of people who rent out a portion of their homes. If you rent the basement apartment in your main residence all winter, but your son lives there for more than fourteen days during his summer vacation, the new rules apply to you.

What about the farm? Do these new rules apply to the farm? Isn't that a vacation-home? It may well be, but these rules only apply in the case of dwelling units. Our weekend farmer was deducting expenses connected with his barn and fields. So he would probably just struggle with the regular profit-motive test. If he tried to deduct the cost of fire insurance or repairs on his farmhouse, it is unclear whether he would be subject to the vacation-home rules, or the regular profit-motive test, or both. Congress has overlooked the weekend farmer, and these questions will have to be worked out by the IRS and the courts.

One final point on vacation-homes (or rental units in your home). If you do not rent the place for more than fourteen days during the year—if it is rented that little—then you can never deduct maintenance or repairs or depreciation. However, the rental income, what little there is, is excluded from gross income.

The Home-Office Deduction. Back in the good old days, taxpayers would use a part of their homes for a variety of business reasons (other than rental). Since a part of the house was used to generate income, a part of the personal expenses of maintaining it became business deductions. These were the home-office deductions.

Suppose you played the stockmarket in your spare time, and you used your den to read the *Wall Street Journal,* study annual reports, clip coupons, and correspond with other investors. Your wife used the den to read, when you were not there, and the kids watched television.

You could then say that you had home-office expenses. A portion of the expenses of maintaining your home were attributable to an income-producing activity—playing the stockmarket. What portion? You figured that out on an area/time basis. You said, "My den occupies 20 percent of my house, and I use it about as much as my wife and kids do. So 20 percent of my house is used half the time for business. Therefore, 10 percent of the expenses of maintaining my house are for business." If it costs you $2000 per year to maintain the house (insurance, utilities, telephone, repairs) you claimed a $200 deduction. Also you depreciated the portion of the house you used for business—another $100–$200 in deductions (you only depreciated 10 percent of it).

Taxpayers who brought work home from the office did the same thing, since then the house was used for their trade or business. So did the woman who sold cosmetics in her home.

The IRS did not take this lying down. Without proof of your wife's reading habits, how did it know whether she used the den as much as you did or four times more than you did? So the IRS said, "The percentage of the time you use the den is the hours you spend in the den divided by *all* the hours in the week, not by just the hours it is used at all." That would bring your percentage down from 10 percent to less than 1 percent. Sometimes the IRS would win, and sometimes it would lose.

Or, not knowing whether you really brought work home from the office, it would allow a deduction only if your job required you to have an office at home and only if you used the den regularly. But then a court would come along and say, "No, it only has to be 'appropriate' for you to work at home, and 'helpful' to your job." That way, lawyers and business executives (and judges) could claim a home-office deduction.

Taxpayers and the IRS spent a good deal of time fighting

over the home-office deduction. Congress, never being one to avoid involvement in obscure and irresolvable problems, jumped into the fight in the 1976 Tax Reform Act. And it promptly slaughtered one of the business taxpayer's favorite tax deductions.

Today, if you use the den to dabble in the stockmarket, forget it. You cannot deduct any of the maintenance costs of your home. Nothing. *Nada. Niente.* Now, that is a pretty clear-cut rule. Taxpayers who use their home for an "income-producing activity" (as opposed to "carrying on a trade or business") get no home-office deduction. It's finished. Dead.

There is still some life left in the home-office deduction for people who use part of their home for a trade or business. If you use your den as headquarters for your business (as the "principal place of your business"), or if you use it to meet clients, patients, or customers, then you get a home-office deduction—*if* you use it *exclusively* and *regularly* for business. So writers or carpenters, who use their den as headquarters, can get a home-office deduction. So can doctors or lawyers who meet with clients in their den even if they have another office downtown. But kick out your wife and kids. The den is off-limits to them. You must pass the "exclusively" test. And use your den for business a couple of nights every week; you must pass the "regularly" test.

What about the guy who brings work home from the office? He's out of luck, unless the work he "brings home" consists of meeting clients or customers *regularly.* If it is just paperwork, forget it. No deduction.

Unless. Unless he has a separate structure on his property, detached from his house. Then he can claim a deduction if he merely uses the separate structure "in connection with" his trade or business. It doesn't have to be his principal place of business. He doesn't have to meet clients there. He just has to use it exclusively and regularly "in connection with" his business, such as bringing work home from the office.

However, there is an additional new rule: His employer must *require* him to bring work home. It must be a condition of employment.

The result of all this is that the only people who can still claim big home-office deductions are the people who are rich enough and important enough to build a little office near their home. Like the corporate executive who always has to work at home and who builds a place behind the swimming pool, with a study (not to mention a bar, and a sauna), which of course is used regularly and exclusively to work at home. Or the man who owns his own business and requires himself to work at home. It was these people whom the Congress said it was aiming at when it shot down the home-office deduction in the first place. Damn if it didn't miss them again.

Congress also decided that it wasn't enough to limit the instances when a home-office deduction could be taken at all. It went on to limit the amount of any deduction you might still take. As with the vacation-home, deductions for home-office costs cannot exceed the income attributable to your home-office after that income has been reduced by the allocable portion of deductions which are allowable anyway, such as interest and taxes.

The effect of this limitation is to wipe out the home-office deduction for practically everybody. Except our friends with the "office" behind the pool. If they make $50,000 and work 10 percent of the time at home (less than one hour per night based on a forty-hour week), they have $5000 in home-office income. Even after reducing that by the mortgage interest and taxes, there should be enough income left over for depreciation (and for the high electricity bill due to the sauna).

Those are the major items for the business taxpayer. As long as you are out to make a profit, you can deduct all the ordinary and necessary expenses of making a profit, including depreciation. But you can't deduct expenses which violate the public policy, and you also have special problems if you are using your business property for personal reasons.

There are other aspects of the business taxpayer's tax liability which need to be looked at. These aspects are best considered in connection with tax shelters. We'll get to that. But first you have to understand capital gains. You won't appreciate tax shelters unless you understand capital gains.

ELEVEN
Capital Gains

What is so special about capital gains that makes them so attractive?

That is an easy question to answer. If you have income which is "subject to capital gain treatment," you pay a tax on only a portion of that income. You can put the other portion in your pocket, and probably it will never be taxed.

What portion goes in your pocket? If you received this kind of income before November 1, 1978, half of it goes in your pocket. November 1, 1978, or after: 60 percent goes in your pocket.

Example: In 1976 you bought some stock for $1000. Today you sell it for $2000. You have a gain of $1000. It is income, to be sure, but income that is subject to capital gain treatment. You take 60 percent of the gain, $600, and you put it in your pocket. (The part that goes in your pocket is called the "capital gain deduction.") It's all yours—tax-free income. Do with it as you please. The other $400? It is added to your other income (your salary, etc.) and taxed at the normal rates.

Capital Assets

What income is subject to capital gain treatment? That, too, is a simple question. Income you get by selling something called a "capital asset." Very good. So what is a "capital asset"? A capital asset is property. Any property. All property. A house, a boat, a painting, stock, a car. *All* property, except . . .

Certain kinds of property are not capital assets.

Business Inventory. The inventory from your business (which, after all, is property) is not a capital asset. If it were, business people might pay tax on only half their income. "Accounts receivable" (which businessmen sometimes sell) are not capital assets either, since they merely represent income from inventories.

Discounted Government Obligations. Those no-interest government securities (such as a savings bond or a treasury bill) that you buy at a discount are not capital assets. Say you buy a "$1000 issue" treasury bill for $940—a 6 percent discount. After a certain period of time, the government will buy back your treasury bill for $1000. The $60 that you make when that security is called at full price is not "income subject to capital gain treatment." Because selling discounted bonds is just one way the government pays you interest. It's only a matter of language. The bonds are not capital assets.

Artistic Creations. A book that you write is not a capital asset. Nothing artistic that you create is a capital asset. You may consider rights in a book that you write—or a painting that you painted—to be property, but if your profit from the sale of these creations could be treated as capital gain, then all the artists would pay tax on only a part of their earnings. The other part would be tax-free. Many artists think that would be proper and fair. But if the artists got their way, everyone would want to earn his living as an artist. Also you would open a Pandora's box of problems. Carpenters would want capital gain treatment on the houses they build and sell. And lawyers would want to sell their opinions of counsel as capital assets. You would see advertisements: "Opinions of Counsel for Sale, Cheap." However, a work of art created by someone else is a capital asset, so if you buy a painting, and then sell it at a profit more than a year later, your gain is income subject to capital gain treatment.

Business Property Besides Inventory. If you are carrying on a trade or business, there are special rules for property besides inventory (such as equipment and fixtures) which you use in your trade or business. As a general rule, this property is treated as a capital asset if you sell it at a gain, but not if you sell it at a loss. If you sell several pieces of property during the year, all of the property is treated as a capital asset if, overall, you had a gain on the sales. But if you had a loss overall, then none of the property is treated as a capital asset. With business fixtures and equipment, capital gain treatment is an all-or-nothing proposition.

For reasons known only to Congress, "publications of the U.S. Government" are not capital assets. I have no idea who sells publications of the U.S. Government, but whoever it is does not receive income subject to capital gain treatment. No tax breaks for selling creations of the U.S. Government.

Apart from the categories of property listed above, all property is a capital asset. Even "income-producing property" (as opposed to inventory or property used in carrying on a trade or business) is a capital asset (unless, of course, it is your own artistic creation). That rental property you own —it is a capital asset.

Long-Term Gains/Short-Term Gains

This all seems simple enough. If you sell a "capital asset" that you owned for more than a year, any profit is income subject to the special capital gain treatment. Part in your pocket, part on top of your other income.

What, then, is so difficult about the subject of capital gains? Why is it so complex that everybody—the White House and the Congress, lawyers and businessmen—wants to simplify the capital gain rules, but nobody knows where to start?

Well, if you have ever glanced at Schedule D of your tax form ("Capital Gains and Losses"), you can see that indeed these rules must be very complex. So here we go.

First of all, there are two categories of capital gain: "long-term" capital gain and "short-term" capital gain. Long-term capital gain is gain from the sale of an asset which you have held *more than one year.* Only this long-term gain qualifies for the special treatment. "Short-term" capital gain is gain from the sale of an asset held for *a year or less.* Short-term capital gain is treated just as plain old ordinary income; the entire gain is added to the rest of your income (salary, savings account interest, etc.) and is taxed in the regular way. So if you buy two paintings (painted by someone else) on June 1, and sell one the following May 30, and the other three days after that on June 2, gain from the first sale is "ordinary income," but gain from the second sale is "income subject to capital gain treatment."

Now what is the point of that? Why complicate matters so? Why draw this distinction between long- and short-term capital gains?

Special treatment for long-term gain has been justified by a variety of reasons. It started in 1921 when, according to congressional documents, people were reluctant to sell their farms or other capital assets that they had owned for a long time because the gains which had accumulated over the years as these properties became more valuable were taxed all at once, at normal rates, in the year of sale. If the gain was large, the taxpayer was pushed into a high bracket, and most of the profit went for taxes.

For example, let us assume that your income is such that you have just entered the 39 percent bracket. You buy a farm in one year and the next year you put up fencing, which increases the value of your farm by $3000 (over the cost of the fencing). If you could sell just the rights to the fencing and have a $3000 gain that year, the extra income would be taxed at 39 percent. Unfortunately you can't do that. So the earnings from your efforts on the fencing just sit there. In the next year, you start breeding cattle. That increases the value of your farm by another $3000. Again, if you could sell the rights in the cattle business for $3000, the extra income would be taxed at the 39 percent bracket. But you don't sell rights in fencing or in cattle. You sell the whole farm—and when you do you have $6000 of income, part of which is taxed at the *42 percent bracket*. The longer you hold the farm, the more the income builds up and the greater the rate of tax when you sell.

Back in 1921, Congress thought that sales were being "seriously retarded" by this condition. The solution, therefore, was to impose a lower rate of tax on gain from the sale of these long-held assets.

This rationale is still used today to justify the special treatment. Long-term capital gain is "bunched income"—income which has built up over many years but is converted to cash all at once and would be taxed at high rates without the special treatment. If it could have been paid to you a little at a time, year by year, the smaller amounts would have been taxed at a lower rate. So it is deemed only proper that this "bunched income" be taxed at a lower rate when you do sell.

Another justification for this special treatment is that long-term gain is, at least partly, the result of inflation, and not the result of accumulated earnings. While your efforts are making your farm more valuable, inflation is also pushing up its value. But an inflationary increase in value is not really income—it does not add to your purchasing power—and so it is not fair to tax it like income. Instead of trying to figure out how much of the gain is due to inflation and how much is accumulated income, the government just taxes the whole thing at a lower rate.

And, finally, there is a justification for the special treatment based on policy. The government wants to encourage people to invest in capital markets, like the stockmarket or the housing and building market, so it taxes the profits from those investments at lower rates.

These and other reasons are used to justify tax breaks for long-term gains. As for short-term gains—well, when you make a pile of money in a short period you can't complain that your income has been building up over the years. You might cry, "Inflation!" but most people agree that if you have gain from an asset held only briefly, you just got lucky on a speculative investment. No tax breaks for good luck.

Granted, these justifications do not really explain why you treat the gain from our two paintings differently just because they were sold three days apart, but Congress had to set the break-off point somewhere. Over the years, this point has been moved backward and forward—two years, eighteen months, six months, nine months. Starting with 1978, it is one year.

So now we know why there are two kinds of capital gain —because for one reason or another Congress does not want you to get walloped by taxes when you sell property you have held for a long time. But if only one kind of capital gain gets the special treatment, why call the other kind "capital gain" in the first place? If there are no tax breaks for short-term capital gains, what is the point of keeping track of them as capital gains?

I'll explain this as we continue, but don't say I didn't warn you.

Short-Term Losses/Long-Term Losses

Once upon a time, you didn't bother keeping track of your short-term capital gains. Back in 1921, when Congress enacted special rules for capital gains, it said nothing about your short-term capital gains. In fact, at that time there was no such thing as a short-term capital gain. There were "regular assets" which gave you ordinary income and there were "capital assets" which gave you capital gain. All property started out as a regular asset, but once you had held it for more than two years—the prescribed time period back in 1921—it became a "capital asset." If you sold a capital asset, you had a capital gain subject to special treatment. It wasn't long-term or short-term. It was either gain from the sale of a capital asset, or it wasn't. If you had held the property for two years or less, you didn't have a capital asset and you didn't have a capital gain, and that was that.

Of course, you didn't always sell capital assets at a gain. Sometimes you sold them at a loss. Up until 1921, if you sold at a loss, you deducted the entire loss from your salary or other ordinary income, just like any other loss, and saved yourself some tax. But when Congress limited the tax you had to pay on a capital gain, it also limited the tax you could save on a capital loss. Fair for gains, fair for losses. Remember, back in 1921 capital gains or losses applied only to property held for more than two years. Losses on property held for two years or less ("regular assets") were still fully deductible. And that's the way it was as of 1929.

Now, you know what happened starting in 1929. Suddenly a lot of people had huge losses on stock which had not been held for two years. People were speculating—buying up cheap stock—thinking that the stockmarket would recover. When it kept going down, they bailed out before two years had passed—in order to deduct the full loss from their salary and other ordinary income. But this was costing the federal treasury a lot of money, and the federal treasury had enough problems at the time. Result: In 1932 Congress put a limit on this kind of deduction—on a loss from stock which was not yet a capital asset (not held two years). A loss from the sale of this short-held stock, Congress said, could *not* be used to reduce taxes on your salary or other ordinary income. It could be used only to offset gain in the same year from the sale of other short-held stock, to reduce taxes on that income. Which was very clever, since in those days there was very little gain to begin with.

This distinction between stock held more than two years and stock held two years or less was the first division of an asset into two categories. Long-term stock and short-term stock.

The next step was that Congress extended this distinction to all assets. After all, you had the right to sell not only your stock, but any of your property, whenever you damn well pleased, and if there were tax benefits in unloading it before two years, why not. At this point the terminology changed. "Regular assets" became "short-term capital assets" and "capital assets" became "long-term capital assets." When you sold short-term capital assets, you had "short-term capital gains" or "short-term capital losses," and the rule for stocks applied. For tax purposes, they had to be balanced out—losses against gains. One would offset the other.

That balancing-out rule still applies today. And that is why you keep track of your "short-term" gains even though they get no tax breaks. Because if you have "short-term" losses, you cannot just deduct them, willy-nilly, from your ordinary income. You deduct them from short-term gains. You balance them out, one against the other.

Question: What if you have no short-term gains to be offset by your short-term losses? What happens to those losses then? We'll get to that.

Which Brings Us to Present Law

The balancing-out requirement for short-term transactions, brought on by the Great Depression, was the forerunner of the more complicated present-day capital gain rules. In 1934 Congress decided to apply the balancing-out requirement to long-term transactions too. It passed a law that long-term gains and losses for the year had to offset one another just like short-term gains and losses. That balancing-out rule still applies today.

Eventually Congress caught up with itself and realized that it had created a totally new category of income—"capital gains and losses"—separate and apart from ordinary income and deductions.

Then Congress had to decide how this new category of income would fit into the other income-tax laws. The objective from the start had been to give long-term gains special tax treatment (while limiting the use of long-term losses). But another objective had surfaced as well, because of the different nature of this income. That objective was to set apart these capital transactions—both long-term and short-term—from other items of income and balance them against one another, drawing a separate, overall picture of your capital transactions for the year. So Congress carried the balancing-out requirement one step further. It said that after you balance out long-term gains and losses against one another, and after you balance out short-term gains and losses against one another, then you balance out what is left —one against the other. If you have a net gain from the long-term balancing, and a net loss from the short-term balancing, then you balance the net gain in the one category against the net loss in the other. The reverse is also true. Net short-term gains against net long-term losses. The one against the other. Once you have done this and drawn your overall picture for capital transactions, then you plug the result back into the regular income-tax laws to determine the tax consequences of your capital transactions.

At the start of this chapter, I said that the special treatment rule applies to "long-term capital gains." Now you can see that the statement was an oversimplification. Because you don't apply that rule or any rule until you have done all this balancing out and drawn your overall capital transaction picture. The special treatment rule applies only if, *overall,* you have a long-term capital gain.

This has become a little complicated, so before moving on, let's take a look at how the balancing-out requirements work. Suppose you sell four capital assets in a certain year with the following results:

Asset #1	$2000 long-term gain	Asset #3	$500 short-term gain
Asset #2	1000 long-term loss	Asset #4	800 short-term loss
Net	$1000 long-term gain	Net	$300 short-term loss

Balancing long-term transactions first, you get a net long-term *gain* of $1000. Balancing short-term transactions next, you get a net short-term *loss* of $300. Under the "overall picture" rule, you then balance your net long-term *gain* of $1000 against your net short-term *loss* of $300. Result: an *overall* long-term gain for the year of $700.

The example above could consist of any combination of figures, depending upon the success or failure of your investments when you sell. Different figures could produce, after balancing out, an overall *short-term* gain instead of a long-term gain. Or, in a good year, you might end up with both a long-term gain and a short-term gain.

The tax rule that applies depends upon the type of *overall* gain. If, after all the balancing out, you have a *long-term gain* (as in the example) then you apply the special rule. Part of the gain goes into your pocket. But if, *overall,* you have a *short-term gain,* that is thrown in with your ordinary income and is taxed at the normal rates. And if, after the balancing, you have both kinds of gain—long-term and short-term—you can't balance them, so the special rule applies to the long-term gain and the ordinary income rule applies to the short-term gain. That is how you determine how your capital gains are taxed.

Obviously, if you sell only one capital asset during the year, there is no balancing. Your "overall picture" is simply the result of that sale. But once you have two or more different kinds of capital transactions, you must balance them out to arrive at your overall capital picture.

What About Losses?

If we had to blame somebody for the complexity of the capital gain rules, it would probably be the speculators of the early '30s. It was their attempt to use their losses from bad investments to cut their taxes which eventually gave us the balancing requirements of today's capital gain rules. I suspect that the speculators did not suffer as much from the enactment of these rules as the rest of us have suffered from trying to understand them, because there is yet another snag.

Congress did not really say that capital losses could be used *only* to offset capital gains. That was just the general rule. Congress promptly made some exceptions to the general rule which still apply. These exceptions tell you what to do when instead of having overall capital gains, you have overall capital losses.

Although Congress was aiming at the speculators in the '30s when it wrote its balancing requirements, it soon became apparent that there were other people in the line of fire. Everybody was into the stockmarket back then, including Mom and Pop. Pop worked at United Success Company until it closed, and he owned two hundred shares of United Success stock which had cost him $2000 and was now worth 20 cents. That was all the stock he owned. Now Mom and

Pop were not really draining the federal treasury. So Congress made an *exception* to its requirement that capital losses *only* be balanced against capital gains, and gave Mom and Pop a break. Congress said that if, after balancing out, Pop had an overall short-term loss (which obviously he did since he had no gains), that overall short-term loss could be used to offset Pop's salary or other ordinary income by up to $2000. This meant that the speculators with overall short-term losses could also offset $2000 of ordinary income, but for them $2000 was a drop in the ocean. The rule was intended to help Mom and Pop, who wouldn't need much more than that.

During World War II, Congress cut the deductible amount of overall losses to $1000, but starting in 1978 this figure is up again to $3000. An overall short-term capital loss —a short-term loss after the balancing—can offset your other income by up to $3000.

So much for *short-term* losses. What if Pop had held his stock for over two years and had a long-term loss? He still wasn't a threat to the federal treasury. So overall long-term losses also became worth a deduction of up to $2000 (today, $3000). But here there was a catch. Since Pop would have had to pay tax on only part of his long-term gain, he could deduct only part his long-term loss. Fair for gains. Fair for losses.

This is still the rule today. Overall long-term losses can offset up to $3000 of ordinary income, but it takes $2 of a long-term loss to offset $1 of ordinary income. To get the maximum deduction of $3000, you need $6000 of overall long-term losses.

Carryovers

The exception to the balancing requirement, permitting a limited deduction for overall capital losses, took care of Mom and Pop. But once the strict balancing requirement had been pierced with an exception, everybody wanted to drive through the hole. In the end, Congress was not as rough on the speculators as it set out to be. A speculator who had a greater loss than he could use in one year under the Mom and Pop exception, Congress decided, could use the excess loss in later years. How? By treating the excess loss as a brand-new loss in later years—short-term or long-term, depending on what it had been in the first year. An unused overall short-term loss, for example, became a brand-new short-term loss in the following year. First it was balanced against any capital gains in the following year. If there were no capital gains, or if some of the excess loss still remained after the balancing, then it could be used to offset ordinary income, up to the deductible limit.

This is still the rule today. Speculators are not banned from using all their capital losses to reduce their taxes; they are only required to use them slowly. Here is an example of how it works.

Suppose this year you have a $7000 overall short-term loss. You offset $3000 in ordinary income this year. That leaves $4000 in losses which you cannot use this year, but which you can use in later years. So you store away that $4000 loss, and next year you bring it out and you treat it as a brand-new short-term capital loss—as though you sold a short-term asset at a loss that year. If there are any capital gains in the second year, it is balanced against those capital gains (first against short-term gains, then against any net long-term gains). If there are no capital gains to be balanced, or if most of the loss still remains after the balancing, then it can be used to offset up to $3000 of income in the second year. Let's suppose you have no gains in the second year, so you offset another $3000 of ordinary income. Now you have used up $6000 of that original $7000 short-term loss, and you still have $1000 left over. So you store away that $1000 until the following year, and then bring it out again and treat it as another brand-new short-term capital loss. You keep storing away those unused losses and bringing them out the next year until you use them all.

If you have a *long-term* loss which you didn't use up in one year, you can also store that away until the following year, and then it is a brand-new long-term loss. You use it first to offset any capital gains (first long-term, then net short-term) otherwise to offset up to $3000 of ordinary income. But remember that you use $2 of long-term loss to offset $1 of ordinary income. So, for example, if you had a $10,000 long-term loss, you would use $6000 of it to offset $3000 of income this year, store away the other $4000, and use it next year first to balance any gains, otherwise to offset another $2000 of ordinary income.

In the tax law, when you store away losses like that and bring them out in the following years, we call that a "capital loss carryover." You carry the loss over to the next year, or the following years, and you use it then.

The $3000 limitation on the use of capital losses raises some technical points.

Suppose your luck deserts you some year and after all the balancing you have both long-term losses and short-term losses in the same year. Can you use each loss to offset up to $3000 of ordinary income, for a total of $6000? The answer is no. You can only offset $3000 of income each year from *all* your capital losses.

This raises another technical point. Which capital loss do you use first to offset ordinary income, the short-term or the long-term? The law requires you to use the short-term loss first. It is to your advantage to do so because your short-term loss will reduce ordinary income dollar for dollar. Eventually you will use it all. But the long-term loss is worth only 50 cents on the dollar if it is used to reduce ordinary income. You get to use your entire long-term loss only if you use it to balance a capital gain. So you are better off saving your long-term loss, hoping to use all of it next year to balance a capital gain, rather than squandering $2 of it just to offset $1 of income. However, if you do not reach the $3000 limit after using the short-term loss, then you must start to squander your long-term loss.

Back to Square One

We have come a long way since that deceptively simple statement that part of your capital gain goes in your pocket. Now let's look at that statement again. In computing your capital gain tax for 1978, you don't necessarily have to put part of the gain in your pocket. On your 1978 return there is an alternative method for computing the tax on your long-term capital gain. It is called the "25 percent rule." Under the 25 percent rule, you simply pay 25 percent of your entire long-term gain as your capital gain tax, regardless of your other taxable income. You don't put anything in your pocket. You just compute your overall long-term gain, take 25 percent, and that is the tax on your capital gain. (This rule applies only to the first $50,000 of gain.)

Is this a better method than the first method of putting a portion of the gain in your pocket? It depends on your tax bracket, but in most cases the 25 percent capital gain tax is used only by people with tax brackets well above 50 percent. Why? Because if your tax bracket is under 50 percent, a tax at ordinary rates on half your gain (or 40 percent of your gain on or after November 1, 1978) will always be less than a 25 percent tax on *all* your gain. For example, let us assume that for 1978 you have a capital gain subject to the 50 percent deduction rule (from a sale before November 1, 1978). Let us further assume that your highest ordinary tax rate is 39 percent. Under the first method, half your capital gain will be taxed at 39 percent. A 39 percent tax on half your gain is the same as a 19.5 percent tax on all the gain—clearly a better deal than a 25 percent tax on all the gain.

Starting with your 1979 return, you don't have to worry

about this alternative 25 percent rule. It has been repealed, effective January 1, 1979. If you have a capital gain after that date, you have no choice but to put 60 percent of your overall long-term capital gain in your pocket and add the rest to ordinary income.

Capital gain from the sale of a home is treated in a special way. If you sell your principal residence at a gain, and within a period of eighteen months before to eighteen months after this sale you buy another home which costs you at least as much money as you received from the sale of the first home, then you pay no tax on your gain from the sale. The tax on this gain is deferred until the time that you sell your home and do not buy another one. Then the gain is taxed under the normal capital gains rules. However, if you are age 55 or over when you sell your home without buying a new one, you can automatically exclude up to $100,000 of any gain which is subject to tax at that time, as long as you have lived in your home for three of the last five years that you owned it. This $100,000 exclusion rule applies to sales made after July 26, 1978.

The Minimum Tax

The Internal Revenue Code provides still another tax—the "minimum tax"—which may have an effect on your capital gain income.

The "minimum tax" differs from the taxes we have been discussing in that it is not a tax on income. It is a tax on deductions—a tax on tax breaks.

You have probably heard that there are high-income people in this country who have learned to manipulate the tax laws so well that they pay no tax at all. To force even these people to pay at least some tax, Congress came up with the "minimum tax." Congress is saying, in effect, "If we can't tax your income because of all your deductions, then we're going to tax some of those deductions. We will add up some of those deductions as though they were income to you, and then we will levy a tax on them."

Some of those deductions. Not all. The "minimum tax" does not levy a tax on all your deductions. Only certain specific deductions which people most frequently use as a means of avoiding taxes. These specific deductions are called "tax preference" items, because they are items which result in "preferential" (i.e., lower) tax treatment. The minimum tax is a tax on "tax preference" items.

There are many tax preference items, some of them highly specialized which affect only a handful of people. For our purposes, we will discuss the two most common.

Under 1978 law (used in filling out your 1978 tax return), you will have a tax preference item that is subject to the minimum tax if your itemized deductions are excessively high. You add up all those deductions which you take to compute taxable income (but you don't count medical-expense deductions or casualty losses). If the total exceeds 60 percent of your adjusted gross income, then the excess is a tax preference item. The reason for this is that some people avoid taxes by giving large sums of money to charity or by investing in tax shelters which produce large interest deductions. Once deductions like these climb to more than 60 percent of adjusted gross income, they start to become a tax preference item, because then you are overdoing it on lowering your income subject to tax.

Another item of tax preference is our old friend—that part of your capital gain which originally went into your pocket—the 50 percent on which you paid no tax at all (or the 60 percent for sales occurring after October 31, 1978): the "capital gain deduction." The capital gain deduction is the tax preference item likely to be encountered by most taxpayers. (Even if you used the 25 percent rule, one-half of your overall long-term capital gain is still an item of tax preference.)

Earlier we said that the part of your capital gain which

goes into your pocket "probably" never gets taxed. Well, probably it does not. But as a tax preference item, it may be taxed under the minimum-tax rules.

The minimum tax is a flat tax of 15 percent. It is imposed on a *part* of the total of all your tax preference items—the total of your excessive itemized deductions and your capital gain deduction and (if you are a wheeler-dealer) your other tax preference items. A *part* of that total. After you have added up all your tax preference items, the total can be reduced. That's right, you add them up and then you cut them back down, before you figure that 15 percent tax.

The total of your tax preference items can be reduced in one of two ways. You can subtract the flat amount of $10,-000. Or you can subtract one-half of the amount of taxes which you are due to pay that year calculated according to the rest of the income-tax laws that we have been discussing. (The tax you are due to pay will include the tax on the taxable part of your capital gain. The "preference" item is the other part—the nontaxable part.) Obviously, you reduce your tax preference total by whichever amount is greater. You then pay a 15 percent minimum tax on the balance.

The minimum tax was designed to penalize big tax avoiders. But it has one unfortunate feature. It can apply to taxpayers who do nothing more than sell their home without buying a new one. If you sell your home at a $30,000 long-term capital gain, the portion of that gain which goes into your pocket is a tax preference item which is subject to the minimum tax.

Obviously, people who do nothing more than sell their homes are not big tax avoiders. And in 1978 Congress changed the law and said that the capital gains deduction from the sale of your home is no longer a tax-preference item. For homes sold after July 26, 1978, the untaxed portion of any capital gain (including the $100,000 exclusion if you are 55 or older) is not subject to the minimum tax.

The minimum tax rules for 1978 are a little complicated.

Unfortunately, Congress has decided that, their complexity notwithstanding, they do not accomplish their purpose. They are too tough on people with relatively small capital gains and too soft on people with huge capital gains. Congress has written new minimum tax rules, effective for 1979. The new rules make the old ones look beautifully simple.

We will not go into these new rules in any detail. Since the capital gain from the sale of your home is no longer a tax-preference item, it is unlikely that you will be subject to these new rules, unless you have large capital gains from other assets, are donating enormous amounts of money to charity, or are a wheeler-dealer. For 1979, there is not one minimum tax but two. One is very similar to the 1978 minimum tax, but it does not apply to capital gains or to excess itemized deductions. The second minimum tax for 1979 applies to the capital gains and excess itemized deductions that are no longer covered by the first one. These rules are intended to collect some tax from people with little taxable income and lots of capital gain. If you are one of these people, you need some tax advice.

We Could Go On

It is only fair to tell you that all of this gets much more complicated. Up to this point we have examined only eight Code sections on capital gain transactions. There are about sixty more sections. But this is as far as we are going. Most of the remaining rules apply to very esoteric transactions (gains from foreign investment-company stock, gains from sales or exchanges of certain patents).

One final point on capital gains and losses. If you sell your house at a gain—or any other personal asset which you did not buy for a business or as an investment—the gain can be subject to capital-gain treatment. However, if you sell assets put only to personal use—a house, a car, or furniture—at a loss, this loss cannot result in a tax benefit. It cannot be used to offset capital gains or as a deduction against ordinary income. This is because the Code does not allow tax benefits for capital losses on property used for personal reasons. Losses on such property are deductible only if they arise from a casualty or from a theft. To obtain a capital loss, the property must be a business or investment asset—stock, cars used in your business, even paintings if you can show you purchased them as an investment. But there is no tax benefit when you sell an old crib at 10 cents on the dollar.

Earlier in the book we thought that it seemed pretty complicated just to figure out gross income—including everything, excluding some things, specifically including others. We looked at the reasons for that and wondered whether they justified the complexity. Now we have looked at the reasons for some very complex capital gains rules. Do these reasons justify the complexity? Or should capital gains and losses just be treated as ordinary income and deductions?

These are questions being debated in Washington right now. Maybe you would like to get in your two cents' worth. By now you probably have as good an understanding of capital gains as many of the people doing the debating.

TWELVE
What's Your Basis?

In the last chapter we saw that the tax treatment of gain or loss from the sale of property is dependent upon several factors: the kind of property involved, the length of time it was held, and other properties sold during the same year. In that chapter we dealt in amounts of gain or loss, for example, "$1000" of long-term gain, "$3000" of short-term loss. Now we turn to the question, Where do these amounts come from? How do you determine the amount of your gain or loss?

Your first reaction to this question might be, "Well, finally something is simple." You might think that the amount of your gain or loss is the difference between what you paid for the property and what you sold it for. In real life that may be true. But not in the world of the tax laws. Under the tax laws, a gain or loss is not the difference between your selling price and your cost. It is the difference between your selling price and a figure called your "basis."

Often, your "basis" is the same figure as your cost. In

fact the Code says, "The basis of property shall be the cost of such property." Clear enough. But that's not all the Code says. It goes on to add, "except [you guessed it] as otherwise provided." So your basis is not always your cost—which is why the tax law refers to basis rather than cost.

Let us examine the nature of basis. Suppose you buy a house to live in for $70,000; you put up $10,000 in cash and take out a $60,000 mortgage. Your basis in the house is your cost, $70,000. So far, so good. If you sell the house more than a year later for $80,000, your capital gain will be $10,000, the difference between your basis and your selling price. Simple.

Now suppose that you are optimistic about real estate, so right after you buy your home, you buy another house, also for $70,000, which you plan to rent out. Again you pay $10,000 in cash and take out a $60,000 mortgage. Your basis is $70,000. Just like your home. Still simple.

Your basis is easily determinable immediately after you buy property because, at that time, your basis is usually your cost. But as you continue to own the property, strange things start to happen to your basis. This is true particularly for income-producing property. And since your gain when you eventually sell is determined by reference to your basis, anything that affects your basis will affect your gain. Which is why, when you own property, you must keep track of your basis.

The Effect of Depreciation

The house you rent out is income-producing property. Therefore, you will depreciate it every year. If the house itself (apart from the land) is worth $60,000 and has a useful life of thirty years, you will depreciate it $2000 each year. (Remember: you cannot depreciate land.) After you take the first $2000 depreciation deduction on your rental house, your basis is no longer $70,000. It is $68,000. We call that your "adjusted basis," because it is your original basis "as adjusted" for depreciation. Each dollar of deduction for depreciation reduces your basis by a dollar. If you sell this rental house a year later for $80,000, you can no longer say, "Well, I paid $70,000, so my gain is $10,000 and that is what I pay tax on." During the year that you owned the house you took a $2000 depreciation deduction, so you must say, "My basis is $68,000, so my gain is $12,000." You end up paying tax on an extra $2000 of gain. (If you ran up some expenses in selling your house, such as broker's fees or lawyer's fees, these expenses reduce the amount of money you are treated as receiving on the sale, but they do not affect your basis.)

Faced with the possibility of additional taxable gain as a result of depreciation, you might ask, "Do I have to take a depreciation deduction?" The answer is, no, you don't have to depreciate your property. You are not forced to depreciate it. But the tax law says that if you are allowed to depreciate, then even if you don't your basis declines as though you did.

Now that does not seem very fair—to have your basis reduced regardless of whether you claim a depreciation deduction. But the fact is, most people want the depreciation and they take it. There are some people, however, who have no use for the depreciation deduction because they have so many other deductions that their income (and their tax) is reduced to zero anyway. When that happens, these people would prefer to take the deductions that don't affect basis (deductions such as interest, taxes, etc.) and forego the depreciation deduction. That way they would keep their basis high and their gain low—looking ahead to when they sell. But under the tax laws, you cannot do that. If you could have depreciated, the Code pretends that you did.

This is not our first encounter with the depreciation deduction. In Chapter 10, on the business taxpayer (which is what you are when you own rental property), we thought that depreciation was a pretty good deal. We remarked on how preposterous it seems to say that property is decreasing in value under the tax laws when in fact it is actually increasing in value. But we admitted that if we can reduce income with a depreciation deduction because our property "declines" in value while all the time it actually grows more valuable—well, that is okay with us. Under the basis rules, the tax laws strike back at that preposterous situation. Sure, you can take a depreciation deduction for this fictional decrease in value, but with it you have to decrease your basis. And you will have to pay more tax when the property is sold. Save now, pay later. Lower basis, more gain. What reduces income today when you depreciate, increases income tomorrow when you sell. (Of course if your property actually decreases in value at the same rate that you depreciate it, then when you sell your selling price will probably be approximately the same as your basis, and there will be little or no gain.)

So the basis rules help the government recoup the tax dollars that it loses from depreciation deductions. Some of those tax dollars anyway. Not all—as we shall see.

Your home cannot be depreciated because it is not business property, so its basis after a year remains $70,000. (Remember, as we saw in the chapter on the business taxpayer, you may use a portion of your home for business purposes —as an office, perhaps, or as a rental unit. In that case, that portion of your home would be depreciable, and then your basis in your home would be affected.)

The Effect of Capital Improvements

The basis on your rental (income-producing) house is affected not only by your depreciation deductions, but also by capital improvements to your property. Let us assume that a year after you buy your rental property, you put on

a new roof which costs you $4000. That changes your basis too. Your basis—reduced to $68,000 by the first year's depreciation—is now increased by the cost of the new roof to $72,000. Capital improvements increase your basis, dollar for dollar, by the amount you spend. If you sold the house immediately for $80,000, your gain would be $8000—the difference between your selling price and your new adjusted basis of $72,000.

Assuming that you do not sell this house—with its new roof—right away, what other strange things happen to your basis?

In the chapter on the business taxpayer, we had a problem with this new roof. We wanted to deduct its entire cost in the year we put it on, but we couldn't do that. We had to "capitalize" it—or deduct the cost over its useful life. The fact is, when you "capitalize" the cost of a new roof, you are merely adding the cost of the roof to your basis in the property, and then *depreciating* the roof over its useful life. "Capitalization" is just another name for depreciation, but is usually used in reference to depreciation of improvements to property, as opposed to the original property itself. So in the year that you add the roof, you take another $2000 "depreciation" deduction on the house and (if the roof cost $4000 and is expected to last ten years) you take a "capitalization" deduction of $400 on the roof. Capitalization deductions, like depreciation deductions, reduce your basis in the property, dollar for dollar.

At this point you might say, "Capitalize the roof, depreciate the house—all this just makes my life more complicated. Once the roof is on the house, why don't I just 'depreciate' the whole thing—house and roof? Why do I have to keep one set of figures for the house, another set for the roof?"

It's a free country and you don't have to. But there are tax benefits to be gained from complicating your life this way. Because the new roof has a shorter *useful life* than the house it is on. A new roof lasts ten years, not thirty. Why

should you depreciate the roof over thirty years, taking a $130 deduction each year, when you can "capitalize" it over ten years, taking a $400 deduction each year? When we make improvements to property which will not last as long as the property itself, we "capitalize" the improvements while we depreciate the property itself.

If our lives are going to be complicated, why not go all the way? If roofs don't last as long as houses, why can't we also depreciate the *original* roof separately from the house and over a shorter period? Why only the new roof? As a matter of fact, you *can* depreciate the original roof (or any other component of the property) separately and over a shorter period. But first you must establish its value and condition. This is no problem when you put on a new roof. But when you buy the house, you don't usually say, "I'll pay $20,000 for the superstructure, $6000 for the roof, $8000 for the bathrooms, and 25 cents for each lightbulb" (although people have been known to do this). So if you wanted to depreciate an original roof separately, you would have to obtain an expert (and honest) appraisal of the value and condition of the roof at the time you buy the house. It might be worth the trouble to get the appraisal if the original roof is fairly new, because no roof will last as long as a house. But if it is an old roof, or in poor condition, its value will be low and there won't be much to depreciate. The cost of the appraisal might exceed the tax savings from any extra depreciation you would get.

Let us continue with our discussion of your rental property. You have added the new $4000 roof, so your basis, which was reduced to $68,000 by the first year's depreciation, is increased by the cost of the new roof to $72,000. You depreciate the house based on its original cost—$2000 each year. You then depreciate the cost of the roof, another $400 per year, making a total depreciation deduction each year of $2400.

The second year of ownership passes. The basis in your house, up to $72,000 after adding the roof, is reduced by $2400 to $69,600. The basis will continue to decline by $2400 each year for nine more years. Then there will be no more depreciation to take on the roof, and the depreciation deductions will revert to $2000 per year, and your basis will begin to decline more slowly again—unless you put on another roof.

When we started to talk about this roof, I said that you added its cost to your basis in the house. But then I went on to say that you kept separate figures and depreciated or capitalized the roof separately from the house. There is no great mystery here. We are just trying to keep track of numbers. If you hold the property for ten years after you add the roof, the cost of the roof has no overall effect on your basis in the house. It might have increased your basis by $4000 when you put it on, but over ten years you depreciate all $4000, and so your basis is reduced by $4000. However, if you sell the property before ten years are up, then the cost of the roof does affect your basis in the house. For example, suppose you sell the house five years after adding the roof. Starting with a basis of $72,000 after adding the roof, the figures for your basis will look like this after five years:

Today's basis		$72,000
Depreciation each year:		
house	$2000	
roof	400	
total	$2400	
× 5 years		12,000
Basis after 5 years		$60,000

If you had not added the roof, your basis figures after five years would look like this:

Today's basis	$68,000
Depreciation each year:	
house only, $2000	
× 5 years	10,000
Basis after 5 years	$58,000

You can see that after five years you have depreciated only one-half the cost of your $4000 roof. You still have $2000 to go. So your basis in your house is higher by that $2000 than it would have been without the new roof. Which reduces your gain when you sell, dollar for dollar, by $2000. You have added the undepreciated cost of the roof to your basis in the house.

One final point on this roof. In the chapter on the business taxpayer, we said that if we patched up the roof instead of replacing it, the entire cost of repatching the roof was deductible currently. Obviously, when you can deduct the entire cost of the repair in the same year that you make it, there is nothing to capitalize. Therefore fully deductible repairs to property have no effect on basis. Only capital improvements.

Improving Your Home

Suppose after the roofer has put a new roof on your rental property, you send him over to your home and he puts a new roof on your home too. Does the cost of the new roof on your home increase your basis? Of course it does; it's a capital improvement. Any work on your nonbusiness property increases your basis if the same work on your business property would have been subject to capitalization. New roofs, landscaping, an addition to your house, a new hot-water heater or furnace—all these items increase your basis in your home. On your own home they cannot be capital-

ized because your home is not business property, but when you sell your home the higher basis will reduce your gain. Which is why you should keep records of capital improvements even on your home—so that you can establish its higher basis if and when you sell.

Problems of interpretation can arise with some improvements. Suppose you decide to replace most of the horizontal pipes in both your houses. Is that a capital improvement which increases your basis, or an ordinary expense which you deduct in the year it is made? It depends on your perspective. For your business property you will say that the cost of the new pipes was an ordinary expense: You had to do it to keep the house in operating condition and to rent it, because then you can deduct the full cost of the work in one year instead of capitalizing it over several years. But for your home, as an ordinary expense, the cost of the work would just be a nondeductible personal expense. So you will say that in your home the work on the pipes was a capital improvement which increases your basis and reduces your gain when you sell. The IRS, of course, might disagree with you on both points, and any two judges on the Tax Court might well disagree with you or with one another.

The Tax Shelter Connection

In the chapter on the business taxpayer, we commented that people were always doing battle with the IRS over whether an expenditure was an ordinary expense or a capital improvement. Now we have seen that, through capitalization, you eventually get to deduct the cost of the capital improvement. If you don't eventually deduct it all (because you sell the property too soon), the undeducted part increases your basis and cuts down your gain on the sale. One way or another, then, the taxpayer gets the tax benefit. So why do we have running battles with the IRS?

One reason, we have already seen, is that you want all that

tax benefit today, not over the years or when you sell. But there is another reason; and this reason becomes particularly important when you plan to sell the property before too long—before you have taken much capitalization. The reason is as follows.

Let us assume that those pipes you put into your rental property cost you $1000, and that you sell the house within a year. Let us further assume that you are in the 39 percent bracket. If you treat the cost of those pipes as a deductible expense, you reduce your ordinary income by $1000 and save $390 in tax. If instead you treat the cost of those pipes as a capital expenditure, you add $1000 to your basis in the house. When you sell, this $1000 addition to your basis reduces your capital gain by $1000. But reducing your capital gain by $1000 does not save you $390 in taxes. It saves you only $195—because capital gains are taxed at only half the rate of ordinary income. You are $195 ahead by taking the deduction. That is why it might be important to treat an expenditure as an expense rather than as a capital improvement. An expense offsets ordinary income taxed at a higher rate; a capital improvement increases basis and reduces capital gain taxed at a lower rate. *Deductions* from ordinary income are worth more tax savings than *reductions* of capital gains.

This difference in value between a deduction and an adjustment to basis also plays an important role in the depreciation deduction. Earlier in the chapter, I said that the government recoups its losses from depreciation by lowering your property's basis under the basis rules. I also said that it does not recoup all its losses. Now you can see why. When it gives you that dollar in depreciation to offset ordinary income, it loses 39 cents in tax. But when it reduces your basis and increases your capital gain by a dollar when you sell, it only picks up 19.5 cents in tax. You come out ahead by 19.5 cents. (Under the 60 percent capital-gain-deduction rule, the government picks up only 15.6 cents.)

There is a name for this phenomenon in which you benefit from the government's loss. It is called "converting ordinary income into capital gain." When you claim a dollar of depreciation, you get a dollar deduction from ordinary income. For tax purposes, you just pretend that you never received that dollar of ordinary income in the first place. That was $1 on which you didn't pay 39 cents in tax. In fact some day you will have to pay a tax on that dollar, because in claiming the depreciation deduction you reduced your basis in the property by a dollar and increased your potential capital gain. So that dollar is sitting there, waiting to be an additional taxable dollar of capital gain. It is taxed when you sell the property. But at that point it is not taxed at the 39 percent rate: It is taxed at the 19.5 percent rate. When you deducted that dollar it came off ordinary income. When you add it back into income, it has been "converted" into capital gain.

This phenomenon called "converting ordinary income into capital gain" is a key principle in tax shelters.

THIRTEEN
Tax Shelters I

There are tax shelters—and then there are *tax shelters*. In this chapter we will talk about both. We are getting into difficult material now. It has to be this way because, after all, we are talking about protecting your income from tax despite Congress's best efforts to tax as much of your income as you can afford to pay. Obviously, it is not easy. I have tried to make the material as simple as the need for accuracy will permit. If you find the going rough, remember that you are not supposed to become a tax-shelter expert, but only understand what these creatures are, and how they work and why. That in itself is not an easy task.

A tax shelter is just what its name implies: an arrangement which permits you to protect or "shelter" your income from tax. There are many ways of doing that.

One arrangement may generate income which is legally exempt from tax, like a tax-free bond.

Another arrangement will produce income which is not taxed for several years, like an individual retirement account.

Still another arrangement will convert income which could be taxed as ordinary income at higher rates into capital gain income taxed at lower rates, such as an investment in depreciable property.

Sometimes a tax shelter will do two or more of these things, or result in still other tax benefits, as we shall see.

This material is not only difficult, it is tricky. Often, when tax-shelter arrangements are at work protecting your income, other rules will also apply which might tax the income you thought you were sheltering. You must proceed with caution. Sometimes these other rules seem completely arbitrary—totally unrelated to the laws you are working under —and sometimes they are. The American taxpayer has become quite adept at avoiding taxes, and Congress has started to fight dirty. We'll talk about that in the next chapter.

The Safe Shelters

There are only two "safe" tax shelters left today—safe in that they are not subject to many surprise rules which prevent you from realizing your objective of avoiding taxes. These two shelters are state and local bonds, which were described in Chapter 3, and individual retirement accounts, which were examined briefly in Chapter 8.

State and local bonds are easy. They are considered tax shelters because the interest they pay is totally exempt from federal income taxation. If the money used to buy tax-exempt bonds were placed in a savings account, it would produce taxable interest. But with tax-exempt bonds all the interest paid goes into your pocket. Not a penny goes to the federal government. (State income taxes may be imposed on this income unless your bonds were issued by your own state.)

For taxpayers with a decent salary and some extra cash that can be tied up for a while, state and local bonds are one of the best tax shelters. If you are married and have taxable income between $16,000 and $20,000, a bond paying only 4 percent tax-free interest would provide you with nearly as good a return as an investment which pays taxable interest at 5.5 percent—because about 25 percent of your taxable interest would go to taxes. So the 4 percent bond pays as good a return as a passbook savings account. A tax-free bond at 5 percent would be nearly as good as a 7 percent taxable investment, such as a time deposit in a savings bank. A 6 percent tax-free bond returns the equivalent of a taxable investment paying about 8 percent—a decent rate for anybody. (These figures are for 1978 rates.)

If your taxable income is higher, the tax-exempt bond yields a greater return because the income it pays would be taxed at higher rates if earned from a taxable investment. To a married couple with taxable income of $20,000 to $24,000, a 4 percent bond is comparable to a taxable investment paying about 5.8 percent—because 28 percent of their taxable interest would go to taxes; to people with $24,000 to $28,000 of taxable income, a 4 percent bond has an effective yield of 6.2 percent. The greater your taxable income, the greater the effective yield of tax-exempts, just because of the increasing percent of interest which would otherwise go to taxes.

When deciding whether to invest in state or local bonds, obviously you must consider other aspects of the investment, not just the tax benefits. You must think about the risk of the investment, the restrictions on liquidity, and other problems. This is true of all tax-sheltered investments.

The exempt bond tax shelter is subject to one surprise rule. You may recall an earlier reference to a part of the Code called "Items Not Deductible." Well, one "Item Not Deductible" is the interest you pay on money borrowed in order to make investments which pay you tax-free income. It's one thing to have tax-exempt income, but to get a deduction by borrowing money to produce that tax-free income, in Congress's view, is going too far. If you buy state or local bonds with cash from a loan, the interest you pay on the loan is never deductible. Moreover, if your investment in tax exempts is substantial (more than 2 percent of your portfolio), the IRS may examine all your investments to determine whether there is a "sufficiently direct relationship" between your other borrowings and your investment in tax exempts. So if you borrowed money to buy stock so that you could use your cash to buy tax exempts, you may still lose the interest deduction. Of if you paid cash for tax exempts, knowing that you would soon need to borrow money to meet other investment expenses, the deduction may be disallowed. If you plan to invest in tax-exempt bonds while you have other investment indebtedness, it is probably advisable to consult a tax expert.

State and local bonds are one tax shelter. Indeed, they may be said to be the ultimate tax shelter because the income is never, never taxed—a characteristic not found in even more sophisticated tax shelters. But when people speak of *tax shelters,* they are not thinking of state and local bonds.

The other "safe" tax shelter is the individual retirement account (IRA)—the bank or insurance account in which you accumulate money for your retirement. You can contribute money to one of these accounts provided your employer does not have a qualified pension or profit-sharing plan in which you participate. If you are single, every year you can contribute 15 percent of your *earned* income (income from working, not from investments) to these accounts, but never more than $1500. If you are married and your spouse does not work, you can establish an account or a subaccount for her. You can then make *equal* contributions to both accounts, up to $875 each, for a total contribution of up to $1750 (but never more than 15 percent of your earned income). If your spouse works, she can make contributions to her own account, provided that she does not participate in an employer pension plan.

Your contributions to an IRA are deductible from gross income (so you benefit even if you do not itemize deductions). The result is that the part of your salary contributed to an IRA is not taxed currently. It is as though you did not receive it that year.

Those contributions you make to an individual retirement account earn interest. But you do not pay taxes on that interest as it is earned. The interest just piles up tax-free.

You pay taxes on the money you put into an IRA, and on the interest it earns, only when you start to withdraw money from the account. Years later, as you take it out, you include it in gross income. Individual retirement accounts are therefore considered tax shelters because taxes are *postponed* on the earned money that you contribute each year and on the interest on that money. Even though you are earning all that income now, you don't pay taxes on it until you use it later on.

Notice that when you withdraw money from an IRA during your retirement, you may have less income each year than you do today, and so you may be in a lower tax bracket. When that happens, you have not only postponed tax on income contributed to, or earned in, an IRA, but you have also lowered the rate at which that income is eventually taxed. Today, that salary or interest would be piled on top of other income and might be taxed at 32 or 36 percent. Years later, it may form the greatest portion of your income and be taxed at no more than 19 or 22 percent. This is another characteristic of a tax shelter: lowering the rate at which a certain part of your income is taxed.

Still, when people talk about *tax shelters,* they are not thinking about individual retirement accounts either.

Owning a home is, in a way, a tax shelter. A home is an investment which often increases in value faster than inflation. Each year it adds to your potential purchasing power —which can be realized at almost any time you choose—but on which you pay no tax until you actually cash in. So a home, or any appreciating asset, is theoretically a tax shelter because the increase in value is sheltered from taxes until you sell.

With a home, you can even avoid paying taxes on the increased value at the time of sale—if you buy another home that costs at least as much as the amount you received from the sale of the first. We have seen that the gain from the sale of one home is not taxed if you buy another home within the period of eighteen months before to eighteen months after the first home is sold, and if you pay at least as much for the second home as you get for the first one. Gain from your first home which goes untaxed does reduce your *basis* in your second home—so if you sold your second home and then rented a home for more than eighteen months, you would be taxed on the gain from both the first and second homes. But as long as you keep buying new homes, that gain just piles up. It reduces the basis in each successive new home, but it is not taxed.

If your home is mortgaged, you have an even better tax shelter. We have already seen how the government helps you pay for a mortgaged home. Those big interest deductions reduce your taxable income and, therefore, the tax which you would otherwise pay. You shelter income from tax and use the tax savings to pay, in part, for your home.

Still, when people speak of tax shelters, they are not thinking of homes.

Tax-exempt bonds, individual retirement accounts, homes—they all shelter income. Why, then, are they not considered *real* tax shelters? The answer is, greed. In these tax shelters, the amount of income sheltered is never very much greater than the amount of money you put up to obtain the shelter, and sometimes it is less. For example, take the $1500 deduction that you get for contributing to an IRA—you pay $1500 in cash to get that deduction, and on top of that you earn only 7 or 8 percent interest each year. You put up $1500, but you shelter only slightly more than that. As for the interest or real-estate tax deductions from your home, they arise because you pay the interest or the tax; it's cash out of your pocket. As for the tax-exempt bond, you put up $1000 cash and all that you shelter each year is $50–$80 in income.

The American taxpayer wants more. He wants to shelter his income at a much lower cost—at a cost in cash which is only a fraction of the amount he is sheltering. Or at no cost. He doesn't want to pay a dollar to shelter a dollar. He wants to pay a dollar and shelter six or seven dollars. He even wants to get his first dollar back, if he can. When you can do these things, you have a real tax shelter.

The Real Shelters

Let's start with that house you buy to rent out. You pay $10,000 cash and borrow $60,000 under a mortgage.

The house generates rental income, but that income is not likely to be taxed because, usually, it is reduced to zero by interest, property taxes, insurance, and other deductible expenses. If the deductible expenses exceed the rental income, you have a loss which you apply against ordinary income (salary, etc.), and then the government helps you pay for your rental property just as it helps you pay for your home.

Suppose your rental home costs $7000 a year to maintain —in interest, repairs, property taxes, and insurance—and you rent it for only $5000 each year. Every year you lose $2000 in cash. But you do not really lose that much because those losses reduce your taxes. If you are in the 39 percent bracket, the $2000 in losses saves you $780 in tax.

Does a $780 tax savings justify a $2000 cash loss? Of course not. But don't forget that your property is probably increasing in value each year. If it increases in value by just $2000 each year, you can recoup your losses whenever you choose to. Let us say you sell the house after a year at a $2000 gain. You get back the $2000 you lost, and you are still ahead of the game because during the year you saved $780 in taxes. Notice, however, that you are not ahead by $780. You must pay a tax on the $2000 gain from the sale of the house. How much does that tax come to? This is a *capital* gain that is being taxed. Under 1978 law the tax comes to $390. Overall, you have made $390.

Let us re-examine what has happened here. On your investment itself you haven't made a nickel. Solely because of the tax laws you have made $390. While you owned the house the government helped you shoulder the burden of that $2000 loss by reducing your taxes by $780. But when you sold the house and recouped your $2000 loss, the government did not make you repay that $780. It made you repay only half of it. We have already given a name to this phenomenon—the "conversion of ordinary income into capital gain." Those losses were losses of ordinary income when you incurred them. When you recoup them, they are in the form of capital gain.

Where are we in terms of our investment? We put up $10,000 in cash, and we made $390. At 3.9 percent, not a very good return. But we are not done.

There is something else about your rental property, and this is what makes it a real tax shelter. The hidden gold in your rental property is depreciation. If the house itself is worth $60,000 and has a useful life of thirty years, you have an additional deduction each year—a $2000 deduction for depreciation. At the 39 percent bracket, this deduction saves you another $780 in taxes in the year that you claim it. So the government has reduced your taxes not by $780, but by $1560—$780 because of your real cash losses, and $780 more because of depreciation.

Now, you already know that when you claim the depreciation deduction, your basis in the property declines by the amount of the deduction. So on your rental house your basis will decline by $2000, which means that your capital gain when you sell will be $2000 greater. That is an extra $2000 which you will have to pay taxes on—but it will be a *capital gain tax*. On the extra $2000 gain, you will pay a tax of $390 (assuming you are still in the 39 percent bracket when you sell). Notice what has happened once again. The $2000 depreciation deduction has saved you $780 in taxes in the year it is claimed, and it costs you $390 in the year that you sell. The conversion of ordinary income into capital gain.

Now where are you? You lost $2000 in cash on the house while you owned it. You recouped that loss when you sold. You reduced your taxes by $1560 while you owned the house. You paid a tax of $780 when you sold. From taxes alone, after a year, you have made $780—a 7.8 percent return on your $10,000 investment.

As a result of the depreciation deduction, the return on your investment has increased by 3.9 percent. Why does that happen with the depreciation deduction? It happens because, to obtain the deduction for depreciation, you do not have to pay out any more money. The deduction is yours just because you own the property. Obviously, if you put up another dollar for each dollar of depreciation, the depreciation deduction would not affect your rate of return. Your tax savings would increase, but so would your investment. The important thing about the depreciation deduction is that it is treated as an expense, and is deductible, even though no expenditure above your original investment has been made. It is an "artificial" expense, but deductible nonetheless.

The "artificial" expense is an important characteristic of a real tax shelter.

There is something else about your rental house which gives it the trappings of a real tax shelter. It is mortgaged. In the financial world, it is often said that your investment is "leveraged." You have a piece of property worth $70,000, but you have put up only $10,000. The bank paid for the rest and, it is hoped, your tenant will pay back the bank. You can see the importance of this leveraging if you re-examine the rate of return on your investment. With an overall tax savings of just $780 and no net income from the investment itself, your rate of return is a decent 7.8 percent. That is because you used only $10,000 of your own money. Investors usually prefer leveraged investments even if they expect the investment to be a success, because it is always better to make money with someone else's money. The attractive thing about tax-sheltered investments is that, if properly leveraged, the tax savings alone provide a decent return, even if the investment itself turns sour. You hope that your house will increase in value by more than $2000 each year, but even if it doesn't, the return on your investment is an acceptable one just because of the tax laws. The tax savings are like a safety factor against your investment risk.

Leveraging and artificial expenses go hand-in-hand in real tax shelters. That $2000 depreciation deduction which you claimed in the first year will also be claimed in the second year, and in the third, and every year for up to thirty years if you hold the property that long. The depreciation on the house over thirty years will shelter $60,000 of ordinary income. At what cost? At a cost of $10,000. Even though you invest only $10,000 cash, you depreciate the entire cost of the house, cash plus mortgage. You put up $10,000 and eventually you deduct $60,000. You put up a dollar, and you shelter six.

A rental house, you see now, is a tax shelter in the true sense of the word. It is a capital asset which converts ordinary income into capital gain. It is depreciable. And it is leveraged.

But there are better tax shelters than a rental house.

Bonus Depreciation,
Accelerated Depreciation,
and the Investment Tax Credit

Let's take the $10,000 you have to invest and, instead of buying a $70,000 house, let's buy you two $35,000 tractors. What are you going to do with two tractors? You are going to rent them out to people who need a tractor only a few weeks each year and would rather rent one from you than buy it themselves. You are going into the equipment-leasing business—into an "equipment-leasing tax shelter."

Now, your first reaction might be, "Hold everything. I don't know a thing about renting tractors." That's okay. Neither do the majority of people who invest in tractors—and we will get to that later.

Equipment leasing is a better tax shelter than rental houses for four reasons, and each reason demonstrates an additional characteristic of a real tax shelter. We will take these reasons one at a time.

Reason Number 1. Equipment has a shorter useful life than real estate. A reasonable economic life for a tractor might be seven years. The shorter the useful life of your property, the greater the depreciation deduction each year. On a $35,000 tractor with a seven-year life, you can take a depreciation deduction each year of $5000. On two tractors you take $10,000 each year—instead of the $2000 deduction you get from your $70,000 house. If you start in the 39 percent bracket (and then come down through the 36 and 32 percent bracket), the $10,000 depreciation on the tractors cuts your taxes by about $3700 each year—the $2000 depreciation on the house, only $780 each year.

Reason Number 2. Tractors are subject to a special bonus depreciation deduction in the first year that you use them.

This is called the "additional first-year depreciation allow-ance." If you buy a tractor, you can take an additional depre-ciation deduction in the year you buy. How much extra? A deduction equal to 20 percent of the first $20,000 of the cost of the tractor, which equals $4000. So when you buy tractors worth at least $20,000, you just deduct another $4000 from your income. (If you are single, your extra deduction is 20 percent of the first $10,000 of cost.)

You cannot take this extra first-year depreciation deduc-tion on your house. It is available only for tangible *personal* property, such as a tractor or a car—not for *real* property. The allowance of extra first-year depreciation is a recogni-tion of the fact that personal property usually declines in value "as soon as it leaves the showroom." It is designed to help you recover some of the cost of your investment in property which is immediately less valuable.

To claim this extra depreciation, you must buy property which has a useful life of six years or more. The reason for the six-year rule is that another purpose of bonus deprecia-tion is to encourage you to buy more property. If you will do that anyway after a couple of years, you get no prodding from Congress. For our seven-year tractors, this six-year re-quirement is no problem.

After you take this extra first-year depreciation, you then depreciate your property in the normal way. How-ever, when you claim that bonus depreciation in the year you buy the property, your normal depreciation deduc-tion is computed a little differently. To determine your normal depreciation deduction, you pretend that the property cost you less money. You pretend that your "basis" for computing depreciation is lower. How much lower? It is lower by the amount of bonus depreciation which you claimed. If you claimed bonus depreciation of $4000 on your tractors, your basis for computing normal depreciation would be $66,000 instead of $70,000. You would pretend that you paid only $66,000 for the tractors, and you would compute normal depreciation accordingly. Obviously, since it reduces your basis immediately, the bonus depreciation in the first year reduces your normal depreciation deductions over the years. But if you want those extra deductions in the first year (because, for example, you have high income that year), this deduction is for you.

Reason Number 3. In addition to the extra first-year depreciation, if you own equipment you can also take "accelerated depreciation." This means that you can depreciate the property more rapidly in the earlier years of its life. (You can take accelerated depreciation on real estate too, but usually to a lesser extent, as we shall see.)

We will spend a few minutes on "accelerated depreciation."

Back in the chapter on the business taxpayer, we were introduced to "straight-line depreciation"—the depreciation of property evenly over its useful life—taking equal amounts of deductions each year. For one $35,000 tractor with a useful life of seven years, straight-line depreciation would be $5000 per year. We said then that there was another kind of depreciation—accelerated depreciation—and here it is. With accelerated depreciation, you don't depreciate the property evenly over its useful life. You take more depreciation in the earlier years and less in the later years.

Why does the government permit you to depreciate your property more rapidly? Accelerated depreciation—as with the extra first-year depreciation—is allowed in recognition of the fact that some property declines faster in value early in its economic life. It also helps you to recover your investment in property quickly, so that you will invest in more property. You should be starting to see that all of the real tax-shelter rules are designed to stimulate investment.

There are many methods of accelerated depreciation. Although these methods lead you into the technical aspects of tax law, they are widely misunderstood, so we will look at some of them.

The fastest method of accelerated depreciation is called the "double declining balance" method or the "200 percent" method. Under this procedure, your depreciation deduction in the first year that you own the property is double what it would be under the straight-line method, but in the following years it steadily decreases until eventually it becomes less than the annual depreciation you would claim under the straight-line method. Here is how it works.

In the first year, you figure out what your depreciation deduction would be under the straight-line method and then you double it, and that is your depreciation deduction for the first year. For a $35,000 tractor with a useful life of seven years, the depreciation deduction under the straight-line method would be $5000 each year. Under the double declining balance method, in the *first* year the depreciation deduction would be $10,000. But from there the depreciation you claim each year under this method starts to go down. The reason for this is that, when you use the double declining balance method, each year you must compute your depreciation deduction all over again, and before you do, you must reduce your basis in the property by the amount of the deduction which you claimed the year before. So in the second year that you own your $35,000 tractor, your basis for computing the depreciation deduction is only $25,000. You figure out what straight-line depreciation would be with that basis ($25,000 ÷ 7, or $3,571.50) and then you double it ($7143): In the second year, your depreciation deduction under the double declining balance method is $7143. And so on. Your depreciation deductions over four years for a $35,000 tractor with a useful life of seven years, under the double declining balance method, would look like this:

Cost	$35,000
First-year deduction ($35,000 ÷ 7 × 2)	10,000
New basis	25,000
Second-year depreciation ($25,000 ÷ 7 × 2)	7,143
New basis	17,857
Third-year depreciation ($17,857 ÷ 7 × 2)	5,102
New basis	12,755
Fourth-year depreciation ($12,755 ÷ 7 × 2)	3,644

and so on, through seven years.

Accelerated depreciation does not get you more total depreciation, it just gets you more depreciation *sooner*. In fact, overall, you get less depreciation under this method. In later years, the amount of the annual depreciation deduction falls below the amount available under the straight-line method. You can see in the example above that, by the fourth year, the deductible depreciation is *less* than it would be under the straight-line method—$3644 rather than $5000. And if you continued the calculations through seven years, you would see that you actually lose about $3300 in depreciation overall. But you do not have to lose that $3300 in depreciation. Once your deductible depreciation falls below what it would be under the straight-line method, the IRS usually permits you to return to the straight-line method for the remainder of the property's useful life in order to fully depreciate it. Depreciation is then calculated on the property's reduced basis at the time, less salvage value.

There are other methods of accelerated depreciation. One is called the "150 percent declining balance" method.

Under this method you figure out your depreciation deduction each year *exactly* as you do under the double declining balance method, but instead of doubling the figure you get under the straight-line method, you multiply it by 1½. Another method is the "125 percent declining balance" method—exactly the same, except you multiply the straight-line figure by 1¼. There are still other methods. In fact, you can use any method which you can persuade the IRS to accept, but none is (or can be) faster than the 200 percent method. You can never multiply that straight-line figure by more than two.

Most property can be depreciated under any accelerated method, as long as it has a useful life of at least three years. For real estate, however, there are special rules. A house (or other residential property, such as an apartment house) can be depreciated under a method as fast as the double declining balance method *only* if it has never before been used as rental property. In other words, if it is new, or in the past it has been only a private residence. But a house which has already been used as rental property is limited to a method no faster than the 125 percent method, and then only if it has a useful life of twenty years or more.

For new nonresidential real estate, such as an office building, a 150 percent method is the fastest depreciation available. For used nonresidential real estate, the straight-line method must usually be used.

Why all these special rules? The government seeks to encourage you to build new buildings (and especially new houses), or to remodel them for investment use, more than to buy buildings already being used for business purposes.

Most of all, the government encourages you to buy non-real property as opposed to houses or buildings. A tractor, for example, not being real estate, can always be depreciated under any method, including the double declining balance method.

So far, we have examined three reasons why tractors provide a better tax shelter than houses. All three involve the depreciation deduction. Tractors have a shorter useful life; they are subject to extra first-year depreciation; and generally they may be depreciated more rapidly. But this is not a rose garden we are turning out with our tractors. There is a catch.

One of the advantages of our rental house was the way in which the depreciation deductions converted ordinary income into capital gain. For the house, those depreciation deductions reduced salary and other ordinary income in the year in which they were claimed. Again assuming the 39 percent bracket, the government reduced our tax by 39 cents for each dollar of depreciation. Granted, the depreciation gave us a lower basis and more gain when we sold the house, but that additional gain was capital gain. Out of every dollar of additional gain, the government took back only 19.5 cents instead of the 39 cents it had allowed earlier. We made 19.5 cents on each dollar of depreciation.

Not so for tractors.

When you sell a tractor, or practically any personal property, any gain which you have solely because the depreciation deductions previously reduced your basis is *not* treated as capital gain. It is treated as ordinary income.

Do not confuse this "paper gain" from a previously reduced basis with "real gain." "Real gain" is always treated as capital gain. If you sell personal property for more than you paid for it, you have a "real gain" and your profit is capital gain. But if your property has declined in value and you have a gain on the sale solely because of a reduced basis from depreciation, this "paper gain" is ordinary income. For example, if you depreciated a $35,000 tractor under the straight-line method, your basis at the end of seven years would be zero. If you then sold it for $7000, you would have a paper gain of $7000. If your tractor were a house, that paper gain would be capital gain. But since it is a tractor, all that gain is taxed as ordinary income. When that happens, it is called "depreciation recapture," and it is the government doing the recapturing. Those depreciation deductions which offset ordinary income in the past are added back to ordinary income when you sell. The income you sheltered is recaptured. (If you took extra first-year depreciation on your tractors, that, too, is recaptured as ordinary income when you sell.)

Does that mean that the tractor is not such a good tax shelter after all? Not at all. Because personal property—such as a tractor or a car—usually declines in value in real life (unlike real estate). When you sell it, you are not likely to have much paper gain, and the amount of depreciation which is recaptured is limited to whatever paper gain you do have. Little gain, little recapture.

It would be better for you if tractors were treated as houses, so that any gain would be capital gain. (In fact, they were treated like houses until 1961.) But the fact that they are not does not make them less attractive than houses as tax shelters. If you have any doubts about that, read the fourth reason why they are in fact better tax shelters.

Reason Number 4. The fourth reason that makes equipment leasing a better tax shelter than rental housing is the biggest reason of all. Equipment is subject to the "investment tax credit."

When we discussed tax credits in Chapter 9, we said that we were reserving discussion of the investment tax credit for now. This is the one for rich people and corporations. It is more complicated than the other tax credits because it is laced with exceptions and special rules. But the basic provisions are not so difficult. Under the investment tax credit rules, you get a credit—not a deduction, a *credit*—against your tax liability in the year that you invest in certain property. What kind of property? Depreciable property. Tractors. Automobiles for your business. Machines. In other words, all depreciable business property. With one exception: buildings. There is usually no investment tax credit for buildings or their structural components. And there is one more condition: The property must have a useful life of at least three years.

Congress has decided that investments in business property are good for the economy and it wants to encourage them. It thinks that they increase productivity, create jobs, and provide more spendable income which in turn stimulates more investment. Whether all of that is true depends on whom you talk to, but the investment tax credit is firmly embedded in the tax laws.

How much of a tax credit do you get for investing in business property? The investment tax credit can never exceed the sum of $25,000 plus 50 percent of tax liability over $25,000 (in 1979, $25,000 plus 60 percent of tax over $25,-000). And it can never exceed your tax liability itself. Within these boundaries, the amount of the credit depends on the useful life of the property. The longer the useful life, the greater the credit. If the property has a useful life of seven years or more, the investment tax credit is 10 percent of the entire cost of the property. In the year that you buy the property, you calculate 10 percent of its cost and take it as a tax credit. If the property has a useful life of only five years or six years, the credit is less; it is 10 percent of only *two-thirds* of the cost of the property. If the useful life is three years or four years, the credit is less still. Ten percent of *one-third* of the cost. And there is no credit at all for buying property with a useful life of less than three years. The Congress may think that long-life assets create more jobs.

Back to your two tractors. We have decided good tractors should last seven years or more. (Remember: It is up to you to assign property a reasonable useful life.) So your investment tax credit is 10 percent of the entire cost of $70,000, or $7000. Not a deduction. A *credit.* In the year in which you buy the tractors, you reduce your tax liability by $7000.

For those of you who are so greedy that you won't pay even $10,000 for $70,000 worth of depreciation—well, you have the investment tax credit. It cuts your investment to $3000, because the government just chops $7000 off your tax liability that year.

That is another characteristic of real tax shelters: The *cost of entry* into the shelter is reduced by the investment tax credit. You get back most of the dollar you put up to get $7 of depreciation.

Now you can see the importance of leveraging. As a result of the investment tax credit, the greater the leveraging, the less the cost of entry. If you pay $10,000 cash for tractors costing $70,000 and borrow $60,000, you are said to be 85 percent leveraged because you have borrowed six-sevenths of the cost ($60,000/$70,000). Your cost of entry is reduced from $10,000 to $3000 by the $7000 investment tax credit. Even better—if you are 90 percent leveraged—if you pay only $7000 cash and borrow $63,000, then the $7000 investment tax credit reduces your cost of entry from $7000 to zero. You pay *nothing* for your depreciation deductions.

So we have seen the fourth, and sometimes the most important, reason why our tractors are a better tax shelter than our house. We cut our taxes by $7000 in the year that we invest.

Now you may say, "The investment tax credit is fine. But the fact is, I never owe $7000 in taxes. My tax liability never exceeds $4000. So what do I want with $7000 of investment tax credit?"

Congress thought of that too.

You remember the capital loss carryover—in which you carried over unused capital losses and deducted them in the next year. If you liked that, you'll love the investment tax credit. Because not only is there an "investment tax credit carryover," there is also an "investment tax credit *carry-*

back." You don't have to wait until next year to use any excess investment tax credit. You can carry the excess credit *back.* How do you carry a credit back? You go back three years and file an amended return for that year in which you claim the unused credit from this year, and you get a refund of the taxes you paid three years ago.

If you still have some credit left over after going back three years, you go to your return of two years ago, then one year ago, filing amended returns and getting refunds of taxes paid in those years. And if you still haven't used up the credit, then you hold onto it and start carrying it forward, like the capital loss carryover, to reduce any taxes you may owe next year or the year after. Or for the five years after that. You can carry your investment tax credit back three years and forward seven years. The government is serious about wanting you to invest in depreciable property.

Before we leave the investment tax credit, we should note the relationship between it and the depreciation deduction. As a general rule, all property has only one useful life. The useful life of property which you assign in order to compute depreciation is also used to compute the investment tax credit, and vice versa. With depreciation, the shorter the useful life you assign your property (within reason) the greater each year's depreciation. But to benefit from the full investment tax credit, you must assign a useful life of at least seven years. If you assign a short useful life in order to generate high depreciation deductions, you may lose part of the investment tax credit. With our tractor, if we assign a useful life of seven years, we get 10 percent of the full cost as a tax credit. We could get away with assigning a useful life of five years to our tractors, instead of seven. We could then depreciate the tractors more quickly. But by assigning a useful life of five years, we get a tax credit of only 10 percent of two-thirds of the cost. We forego $2400 of investment tax credit. So you must decide what you want: Do you want a big tax credit this year, or do you want greater amounts of depreciation over a shorter period of time? It depends on whether you have a high tax bill this year, or whether you expect to have high income over the next few years.

Dollars and Cents

With our four reasons that make tractors a better tax shelter than houses, we have now seen all the building blocks of real tax shelters. There are many kinds of tax shelters, but they all consist of the elements we've examined—conversion of ordinary income into capital gain, artificial losses, short useful lives, extra and accelerated depreciation, leveraging, and low cost of entry. Soon we will look at other aspects of tax shelters—the dangerous aspects. But first let's see what these shelters mean in terms of dollars and cents. Tax shelters can produce surprising results when they are analyzed as investments—and an asset which *decreases* in value can be as good an investment as one which *skyrockets* in value, solely because of the tax laws.

Compare the tractors and the house. Assume that, for both properties, income is exactly offset by actual expenses.

Let us review what we already know about these two investments. Both assets cost $70,000, but the tractors have a shorter useful life—seven years instead of thirty. Even if you just take straight-line depreciation (and no extra first-year depreciation), the tractors will produce a deduction of $10,000 per year ($70,000 divided by 7); the house, only $2000 ($60,000—excluding the land—divided by 30).

Now compare their effect on your taxes. Assuming that you are in the 39 percent bracket, the tractors, with their $10,000 yearly depreciation, save you about $3700 in taxes each year. This is almost $26,000 over the seven-year life of the tractors. The house, with yearly depreciation deductions of $2000, saves you only about $800 in taxes every year—or $5600 over the same seven years—and it takes thirty years to obtain all the tax benefits.

Now look at what it costs you to obtain these tax benefits. The tractors cost you $3000 if you were 85 percent leveraged, because you got a $7000 investment tax credit. For the house there is no investment tax credit, so if you were 85 percent leveraged, you paid $10,000 to get in.

On the other hand, the house will increase in value, while the tractor's value will decline. After seven years, the tractors together may be worth only $7000, while the house may be worth $110,000. Does that make the house a better investment? Not necessarily.

Compare the overall cash return on both properties after seven years. First the tractors. After seven years you have paid off the mortgage with rental income from the tractors. Now you sell the tractors for $7000. Your depreciation over seven years has reduced your basis to zero, so you have a gain of $7000. Since the gain is a paper gain, the result of a lower basis due to depreciation, the entire gain is recaptured as ordinary income. This means you would pay a tax on that gain of about $3000. That leaves you with $4000 after the sale. Your total cash return (on the $10,000 you put up) from the tractors looks like this:

Tax savings from depreciation	$26,000
Investment tax credit	7,000
Net proceeds from sale	4,000
Total	$37,000

Your cash return from the tractors, after seven years, is $37,000.

Now the house. After seven years, you sell the house for $110,000, $40,000 more than you paid for it. But $2000 of depreciation for seven years has reduced your basis in the house to $56,000, so your capital gain is $54,000. Let us say that that much gain pushes you into a high tax bracket and, after 60 percent of it is deducted, results in an additional tax of $13,500. You have $26,500 profit left after taxes ($40,000 less $13,500). Your cash-return picture from the house looks like this:

Tax savings from depreciation	$ 5,600
Investment tax credit (not available)	–0–
Net proceeds from sale	26,500
Total	$32,100

Your cash return from the house, after seven years, is $32,-100.

So over a seven-year period the tractors are a better investment than the house, solely because of the tax laws. Even though the tractors decline 80 percent in value, and even though the house increases in value by more than 50 percent, still you do better with the tractors just because of the tax laws. (The figures will change slightly under 1979 law, but the principle remains the same.)

Of course if you held the house longer, its value should go even higher and the tax savings from depreciation would add up to more dollars, and eventually the house would bring a higher return.

Your choice of tax shelters, therefore, depends on your objectives. If you wish to shelter a lot of income now, you buy the tractors. If you are looking for a modest tax shelter (because you pay only modest taxes) and a bigger gain over the long run, and you don't mind tying up the original investment on which there is no tax credit, you buy the house.

If you can't decide which investment you prefer but are prepared to tie up $7000, you might make both investments. By leveraging the tractors at 90 percent, you invest $7000 and the government gives you a $7000 tax credit. If you can leverage the house at 90 percent, you take your $7000 tax credit and use it as a down payment on the house.

It all looks pretty good, doesn't it? Sometimes it *is* good. But remember that we are dealing in ideal circumstances.

Eighty-five—or 90—percent leveraging. Income offsetting expenses. House and tractors always rented. Our house doesn't require extensive repairs. Our tractors don't need new engines. Apart from the tax aspects of these investments, there are obviously other very real problems to think about.

There are also other tax problems. In this chapter we have covered the helpful tax-shelter rules—the ones that save you tax. Now let's turn to the ones that trip you up.

FOURTEEN
Tax Shelters II:
The Congress Fights Back

Congress does not intend to write tax laws which enable you to make money on investments just by avoiding taxes. When people invest, Congress expects them to profit because they make good investments and manage them properly—not because they weave their way through the tax laws, collecting their profits only at the expense of the federal treasury. So there are more tax-shelter rules—special rules intended to prevent you from profiting solely by saving taxes. These are rules which prevent you from sheltering as much income as you had hoped to. Once you start playing with real tax shelters, you must watch out for the special rules.

Recapturing the Investment Tax Credit

One of the special rules is the "investment tax credit recapture." It is designed to prevent you from buying property just to obtain a tax credit. Let's face it—if you got a tax credit just for buying property, each year everybody would buy a piece of property, claim the credit, and then turn around and sell the property right away. The "investment tax credit recapture" rule prevents you from doing this.

We know that if you assign a useful life of seven years to your tractors, the government gives you a tax credit: 10 percent of your full cost. But under the recapture rule, the government holds you to your word. If you sell the tractors before seven years, it wants part or all of its credit back. When you sell you must recompute the investment tax credit based on the length of time you actually used the property. If you sold in five years, the government would say, "If you declared a useful life of five years in the first place, your credit would have been 10 percent of only *two-thirds* of your cost, or about $4600, not $7000. So now that you have sold early, we want the overestimated credit back." In the year of sale, your *tax liability* (not just your income) would be increased by $2400. You pay back $2400 of the $7000 credit that you took when you bought the tractor. That is called the "recapture" of the investment tax credit.

If you sold the property in two years, or right away, the government would recapture all $7000 of the credit because there is no credit for property with a useful life to you of less than three years.

So you cannot buy property just to avoid taxes. And when you take the investment tax credit, you must plan ahead on how long you really expect to hold the property.

Recapture of Accelerated Depreciation on Real Property

We have seen that when you depreciate a house, the deductions offset ordinary income. Your basis in the house is reduced by the depreciation you claim, so you may have more gain when you sell. However, that gain is capital gain which is taxed at a lower rate than the income the depreciation offset—so overall you come out ahead. You have converted ordinary income into capital gain.

We have also seen that this phenomenon does not occur with tractors. When you depreciate a tractor you cannot convert ordinary income into capital gain. With a tractor any paper gain on a subsequent sale is not capital gain, but ordinary income. We called that "depreciation recapture." We stated that this "depreciation recapture" rule applies to personal property, not to real property—not to your house. That is a correct statement provided you depreciate your house under the straight-line method. But we know that you can take accelerated depreciation for your house if you want to. If you do, the depreciation recapture rule comes into effect.

The rule on recapturing accelerated depreciation on real property works like the depreciation recapture rule for tractors. Depreciation claimed in earlier years is added to ordinary income when you sell. For the tractors, *all* the depreciation you claimed earlier was added to ordinary income when you sell. But for real property, only a *portion* of the depreciation is added to ordinary income: the "accelerated" portion—that additional depreciation you claimed over the years by using an accelerated method of depreciation instead of the straight-line method.

This is how it works. Suppose you own a $70,000 new house ($60,000 of which is depreciable) for three years. Assigning a useful life of thirty years to the property, let us compare the amount of depreciation you would claim under the two methods: the double declining balance method, and the straight-line method.

	Double Declining Balance	Straight-line
Year 1	$ 4,000	$ 2,000
Year 2	$ 3,733	2,000
Year 3	3,484	2,000
Total over 3 years	$ 11,217	$ 6,000

The "accelerated" portion of your depreciation is $5217 ($11,217–$6000). If you sold the house after three years, you would have to add $5217 to ordinary income. That extra depreciation you claimed while owning the property is recaptured when you sell. The government does not permit you to pile up huge depreciation deductions and then dump your property.

Note that as you hold the house longer, the amount of accelerated depreciation declines, and at some point in the future the accelerated method has not, overall, produced more depreciation than the straight-line method. If you sold then, there would be no accelerated depreciation to recapture.

Does this recapture of accelerated depreciation rule apply to tractors? Of course not. When you sell a tractor you recapture *all* depreciation, accelerated or straight-line.

There are a number of wrinkles in the recapture rules for real property. For example, if the amount of gain on the sale of your house is less than the amount of excess depreciation which you have claimed over the years, you recapture only the smaller amount. Also, the rules change slightly for accelerated depreciation claimed before 1976. In addition, certain kinds of real property are not subject to the recapture rules. We cannot go into all the wrinkles here. What is important is to understand that when you sell real property which has been depreciated rapidly you have recapture problems which must be considered.

The Limitation on Interest Deductions

There is another special rule for interest deductions. We have seen that if your rental property loses money every year, the government helps you absorb the loss by letting you reduce your ordinary income (salary, etc.) by the amount of the loss. If you recoup your losses by selling at a gain, the gain is taxed at capital gain rates so you still come out ahead. (The recapture rules apply only to the part of your losses attributable to depreciation deductions.) But under the special rule for interest deductions, if the losses on your property are due in large part to high interest payments, some of those losses may not be deductible.

Suppose your rental property was a building that cost $500,000, instead of a house costing $70,000, and the interest payments on the mortgage came to about $50,000 each year, during the early years of the mortgage. The Code limits the amount which an individual taxpayer can deduct in any one year for interest paid on money borrowed to make an investment. (There is no limit on deductions for interest paid for personal assets, like your home, only on deductions for "investment interest.") The limit is $10,000 plus something called "net investment income." What is net investment income? It is your net income from the property, after you have taken depreciation and all other deductions *except* interest. Figure your net income from the property (disregarding interest paid), and then add a flat $10,000. The total is the maximum amount of interest you can deduct in that year. The government will help you pay for some of your losses, but there are limits.

Example: If your $500,000 building was rented for $70,-000 per year, and your deductions for maintenance, insurance, property taxes, and depreciation came to $40,000, your "net investment income" would be $30,000. That figure, plus the flat $10,000, is your limit—the most interest you can deduct. In this case, $40,000. If the interest amounts to $50,000, you lose $10,000 in interest deductions that year.

Any interest not deducted because of the limitation can be carried over to the next year and treated as interest paid in that year. But you may have the same problem in the next year, and you may have to wait many years before you use those excess interest deductions. (You should be able to use them eventually, however, because as you hold mortgaged property longer, you start to pay less interest and more principal—so that in later years you have little interest to deduct and can start to use the excess interest from earlier years.)

We didn't discuss the limitation on the deduction of investment interest earlier, when we talked about the vacation-home which you treat as rental property. You would have to buy an enormous vacation-home before you could lose part of the interest deductions. But the limitation applies to all business investments, including rental property used as a vacation-home.

The Minimum Tax

Still another rule to bear in mind in tax-shelter planning is the "minimum tax"—that tax against tax breaks that we discussed in Chapter 11 on capital gains (total your "tax preference" items, subtract $10,000 or else one-half of regular taxes paid, and take 15 percent of the balance). We return to that now because we have been discussing two other items of "tax preference."

One of these items is the "accelerated portion" of depreciation *each year* on leased personal property. On your tractors. The amount of depreciation each year which is in excess of straight-line depreciation is a tax preference item. Earlier we saw that, when you take accelerated depreciation on your tractors, the amount of total depreciation for the first few years is greater than it would be under the straight-line method. Now we see that each year that excess amount of depreciation is added to your other tax preference items for the year (excessive itemized deductions, the capital gain deduction) and may be subject to the minimum tax.

The other tax preference item we have been discussing is the accelerated depreciation that you take on real estate, for example, on your rental house. Note that for real estate this is the second pitfall of accelerated depreciation. Earlier we said that if you *sell* your house too early, you include in your ordinary income in the year of sale the total "accelerated portion" of your depreciation for the years you owned the house—the excess of the total accelerated depreciation claimed over the total of the straight-line depreciation you could have claimed. Now we find that in any one year the "accelerated portion" of your depreciation for that year is also a tax preference item. You add that accelerated portion of your depreciation to your other tax preference items for the year. If they exceed $10,000, or one-half of the regular taxes you pay for the year, the 15 percent minimum tax will apply to the excess.

The "At Risk" Rule

There is another special rule which applies when you invest in certain tax-shelter assets. It is called the "at risk" rule. When people say that the tax-shelter rules have changed, they are thinking of the "at risk" rule. It is the biggest special rule of all.

Some American taxpayers were not satisfied with purchasing $70,000 of depreciation deductions for $7000, or even with getting their $7000 back under the investment tax credit. These tax benefits were tempting, but the fact remained that, having bought two tractors, investors were responsible for paying for two tractors. They went $63,000 into debt. It was hoped that the tractors themselves would pay off the loan, but the investors were on the line for $63,-000 if something went wrong. A $33,000 tax benefit didn't look so great compared to $63,000 of personal liability.

So they arranged to cut their risk even further. They developed a special, low-risk system for financing the tractors: the "non-recourse loan."

A non-recourse loan is exactly what you might think. It is a loan under whose terms the lender has no "recourse" against the borrower. If the borrower doesn't pay back the loan, the lender cannot sue him. The borrower has no personal liability for paying the loan back.

Now why would anybody lend money to someone else and not hold him personally responsible for paying it back? In fact, there are many reasons why that might occur, and most of them involve questions of sophisticated high-finance transactions. To focus on a simple reason, put yourself in the position of a tractor manufacturer or a tractor dealer who wants to sell tractors. Somebody comes to you who knows something about tractors and offers to buy one for $35,000. He's willing to put down $3500 cash, but he expects you to finance the balance with a loan repayable over seven years. In addition to that, he won't be responsible for repaying the loan. All he will do is put up the tractor as security. If he doesn't pay you back, you take back the tractor.

Do you throw him out of your tractor shop? Well, you know something about tractors too. You know that a tractor will probably last seven years, and that it will not decrease in value as quickly as the loan is scheduled to be paid off. So if payments are not made, you would be satisfied if you can take back the tractor and sell it to someone else. There might be more paperwork than you would like, but your money is basically secure. In any event, this person knows a lot about tractors and will probably be able to rent his tractor out and pay his bills to you. On the whole, since you want to sell your tractors, his proposal seems worth the risk.

The result is a non-recourse loan.

Now put yourself into the position of the purchaser. You pay $3500 cash, and the government gives you a $3500 tax credit. Your tractor produces a depreciation deduction of $5000 a year, saving you $2000 a year in taxes (at the 39 percent bracket). Even if the tractor operates at a $1000 loss, you are $1000 better off, thanks to depreciation. If things fall apart, you have no personal liability. You just lose the tractor, which didn't cost you anything anyway.

Congress decided that it was one thing to permit tax breaks when the investor was taking a chance on losing a great sum of money. But when his risk was limited, excessive tax benefits were inappropriate. The result was the "at risk" rule.

Under the at risk rule, the greatest amount of loss in any year (income less all deductions) which you can claim on an investment in certain kinds of property is the amount of money which you have "at risk." In the above example, the investor has only $3500 at risk because he has no personal liability on the loan (the fact that he gets back his $3500 under the investment tax credit does not alter the fact that he put it up in the first place). If income from the tractor offsets operating expenses, he still has a $5000 loss (from depreciation). But under the at risk rule, he can deduct only $3500 of that loss from his salary or other income. So he is not sheltering as much income as he planned to.

What about the losses he cannot deduct? Like unused capital losses or excess interest deductions, any losses not used in one year because of the at risk rule can be carried over and treated as a new deduction in the next year. So our tractor owner would use his leftover $1500 loss as a deduction from tractor income in the following year. But the at risk rule will apply next year too. By next year he might have paid off $1000 in principal on the loan—thereby increasing the amount he has "at risk" from $3500 to $4500. And, with smaller interest payments, he might lose only $4000 the next year. But the $4000 loss next year, plus $1500 carried over from this year, gives him total losses next year of $5500. So with only $4500 at risk, he must carry $1000 over to the following year. And on it goes. It can take years to use all the losses to shelter your other income.

The at risk rule, more than any other special rule, was intended to eliminate the tax shelters which Congress found most offensive—those financed with non-recourse loans. For individuals, it at first applied only to investments in certain kinds of assets—equipment, oil and gas properties, motion picture films, and certain farming operations—because these properties are depreciated quickly and are often financed with non-recourse loans. But then taxpayers began to find other kinds of property for tax shelters, so starting in 1979 the "at risk" rule applies to investments in *all* assets except real estate.

These special rules start to make tax shelters complicated and dangerous if you don't know what you are doing, particularly when more than one special rule applies. For example, suppose in one year you find yourself exposed to the excess interest deductions rule (you paid $40,000 in interest but your deductible limit was $30,000) and you also have losses in excess of the amount you have "at risk." Which limitation applies first, the interest limitation or the at risk rule? If you think about it carefully, you realize that the interest limitation rule applies first, because the losses which you might not be able to claim under the at risk rule consist in part of the interest deductions. If you paid $40,000 in interest but can deduct only $30,000 because of the interest limitation, you deduct $30,000 in interest this year and carry $10,000 over to next year. If using the $30,000 interest deduction together with your other expenses results in an overall loss of $15,000 this year, but you have only $10,000 at risk, then you can claim a loss this year of only $10,000, and you must carry the remaining $5000 in losses over to next year and treat it as a deductible expense then. The result is you carry over $15,000 of unused deductions ($10,-000 in excess interest and $5000 in unusable losses), and before the next year even starts, you have $15,000 in deductions. If you have excess interest and unused losses in the next year, your carryovers will start to pile up. You must plan ahead to avoid something like that. Otherwise your tax shelter does not accomplish its purpose.

Partnerships

You may be starting to feel that tax shelters are a bit intimidating. First you must wade through all these tax laws, balancing investment objectives with sheltering objectives, and watching out for the surprises. Then you must go out and find a good investment, and obtain financing for it. Then you must manage and maintain the asset—i.e., getting the tractor repaired, renting it out, or hauling it around. After you look at all these problems, you may feel that you don't really care to spend your nights and weekends struggling with the tax laws. Also, you do not enjoy responding to want ads for your tractors. And, as you said at the very beginning, you don't know anything about tractors anyway.

A lot of people who needed tax shelters shared your sentiments. It was too complicated and too much work for just one person. So people started to form partnerships.

Why partnerships? The partnership is a perfect medium for tax-sheltered investments for one good reason: Under the tax laws, for all practical purposes, it does not exist. Income earned by a partnership flows straight through to the partners and is income to them. Losses of a partnership are losses for the partners. Under the tax laws, all a partnership does is keep track of things. It adds up its income, subtracts its deductions, and takes its depreciation. But it doesn't pay any tax. Instead, the partners account for its gains or losses (even for its investment tax credit) on their own tax returns.

So, reluctant to undertake so much work alone, you and your neighbor formed a partnership—50-50—and the partnership bought two tractors. Under state law your partnership was a recognized, legal entity; it could own property and manage it. Because of the partnership, you and your neighbor, as partners, were each responsible for paying for the tractors, and neither one of you could sell them without the permission of the other. Under state law the partnership existed and was subject to special rules applicable to business entities carried on as partnerships—rules which protected you from your partner, and vice versa. But for purposes of the tax laws, your partnership was hardly there. If the partnership made $10,000, you and your neighbor each had $5000 in income to pay tax on. If it lost $10,000, you and your partner each claimed a $5000 loss.

The partnership proved to be a good way to get someone to help you bear the burdens of investing in a tax shelter. You could both struggle with the tax laws, and you could take turns renting the tractors.

There was just one little problem. The only way to cut down on the work was to limit the investment to what you would have invested in by yourself—two tractors. After all, if you bought four tractors there was no less work for either of you just because you were in the partnership. However, the problem with buying just two tractors was that for each of you the tax benefits were cut in half—and the whole point was to get the tax benefits. So unless your neighbor was a tax lawyer who grew up on a farm and could manage four tractors, forming a partnership with him wouldn't have gotten you very far.

The solution, obviously, was to hire somebody to take care of the tractors and to figure out all the tax problems, and then tell you at the end of the year how much you could deduct. Unfortunately, for just you and your neighbor, that cost too much money. If you were going to pay a manager, you would have to deal in volume. So you went out and found eight more people, and the ten of you formed a partnership and bought twenty tractors, and each of you put up a little money to hire somebody to run your tractor business. The manager rented the tractors, he maintained them, he kept all the records of income and expenses, and every January he told you how much you could deduct for the previous year.

Today, you don't have to form your own partnership with your neighbor and eight friends. You don't even have to go to that much trouble. People form them for you—big partnerships. Two people who know something about tractors start a partnership and they manage it. They call you up and say, "For $7000 you can become a partner in this partnership, and we will use your $7000 to buy two tractors, and you will get the tax benefits from those tractors and pay us a small management fee." Then they make the same arrangements with forty other people. Soon they have built themselves a total management fee that is not so small, but you don't care because your share is small and it's deductible anyway. If you need a tax shelter, the management fee is worth the trouble it saves to get into one.

These two organizers are not always tractor experts. They may be aviation fanatics. So they decide to get five hundred people to invest in a Boeing 727 and rent it out. Instead of having a full interest in two tractors, you have 1/500 of an interest in one Boeing 727 which provides you with the same tax benefits. Maybe they would decide to buy a fleet of trucks, or a fishing boat, or railroad cars, or any other kind of asset which can be leveraged, is depreciable, and has a fairly good chance of producing enough income to cover its own operating costs.

When people start partnerships like this and sell shares to you and other people, they call it a "syndicate."

Syndicates made it easy for people to get into tax shelters. They also made it easy for people to start to abuse the tax-shelter rules, and it was because of syndicates that changes started to occur and rules like the "at risk" limitation began to take shape. You may have been wondering why the government would go to so much trouble to put the reins on some industrious person claiming a $3000 or $5000 loss each year. Had losses in tax shelters stayed that small, the government probably would not have clamped down. But once syndicates started to form, the amount of money involved became far greater.

A popular syndicated tax shelter was the motion picture

shelter. A syndicate would agree to buy the rights to a movie for, say, $1 million. It would pay $100,000 cash down (a sum which an individual investor might not put up by himself), and make a non-recourse promise (a non-binding promise) to pay the remaining $900,000 out of royalties from the movie, but only if royalties exceeded $100,000. The people who owned the rights to the movie were willing to do this because a film is always a speculative moneymaker, and they weren't sure that the film would earn even $100,000. If it flopped, they at least had $100,000. If it was a hit and earned millions, then they would participate in the profits up to $1 million. For them, it was a no-lose transaction.

The syndicate would then sell rights in the film to ten investors for $10,000 each. For the ten investors it was also a no-lose transaction. This was because the cost of the film to each of them was $100,000 (one tenth of $1 million), and because a film has a short useful life (maybe two years) especially if it fails. Each investor therefore had $100,000 of depreciation which he could claim over two years. If he was in the 40 percent bracket, he cut his taxes by $40,000 in just two years—all for a $10,000 investment. Even if the film didn't earn a dime, he had a $30,000 profit. If the film was a success, so much the better; the syndicate could always go out and find a turkey to offset the income from a smash.

It was abuses such as the movie tax shelter that prompted Congress to enact the at risk limitation. If all you put up is $10,000 and if that is all you have "at risk," all you can deduct in any one year is $10,000.

Once the syndicates got going, they discovered that they could perform tax-avoiding magic. Non-recourse loans were not always available for the assets in which a syndicate invested, but the syndicators were able to offer their investors limited personal liability anyway—as though there were a non-recourse loan. This was accomplished through an organizational device called the "limited partnership." The partnership laws of all states recognize two kinds of partners in a partnership: "general partners" and "limited partners." General partners manage the partnership and are fully responsible for the partnership liabilities or losses. But limited partners are just investors, and are responsible only to the extent of their investment. If a limited partner contributes only $10,000 to a partnership, that is all he stands to lose. He cannot be sued for more than the $10,000 he has already paid into the partnership. A limited partnership interest is like a non-recourse loan. You put up some cash, and all you can lose is the cash you put up.

Every partnership must have at least one general partner because somebody has to manage the partnership and be responsible for it. In most syndicates, the syndicators would be the general partners. The investors would all be limited partners. If things didn't work out, the investors' liability would be limited to the amount of their investment. Of course for the most part, the tax laws didn't recognize partnerships in the first place, so the limited partners still shared fully in the income and deductions of the partnership.

Why would the syndicators be willing to shoulder most of the liability? Because when they analyzed the potential liability, they discovered it was not that great. In the kinds of businesses which attracted the syndicates, only two things could go wrong. Your tractors could explode, or your Boeing 727 could crash, and you would be a defendant in a personal injury suit. But you could buy insurance to protect yourself against that. Or the whole deal could go sour, and you could lose a lot of money. But the syndicators knew what they were doing, and through careful planning and financing, they could minimize the risk of economic failure. And if the business did fail, the partnership owned the kinds of assets a bank would foreclose on—real estate, airplanes, heavy equipment. As a practical matter, it was easier for everybody—the bank, the investors, and the syndicators—for the bank to foreclose on the assets rather than sue the partners.

Most syndicates started to take the form of limited partnerships. Even without non-recourse financing of the assets of the partnership, the investors were still getting all of the tax benefits with limited investment and limited risk. The result? Congress decided to apply the at risk rule to limited partnership interests. If you are a limited partner in a partnership, the amount of partnership losses that you can deduct yourself are limited to the amount of your investment in the partnership. This rule applies to investments in *all* limited partnerships, regardless of the asset in which the partnership itself invests. In the case of individual investors, the at risk rules were only necessary for investments which could be financed with non-recourse loans. But when you bought shares in a limited partnership, that was the same thing as a non-recourse loan. So the at risk rule was made applicable to limited investments in all partnerships. The result is that, if you invest $10,000 in a limited partnership which is itself investing in *any* asset, the greatest amount of loss which you can claim in any one year is $10,000.

There is one exception to the at risk rule as it applies to limited partnership interests. If the partnership invests in real estate, there is no at risk limitation on tax benefits even if you are a limited partner. The at risk rule became law at a time when the real-estate market was in a shambles, and so an exception for real estate was carved out to encourage more investment. We have seen that, for individuals, the at risk rule at first applied to investments in certain assets, such as equipment. We have also seen that, for limited partnerships, it applies to all limited partnership interests, regardless of the asset purchased by the partnership (except for real estate). What happens if you are a limited partner in a partnership that invests in the kind of asset subject to the at risk rule for individuals (such as a tractor)? Does the at risk rule apply twice—once because of the asset and once because of the limited partnership? No. If the at risk rule applies because of the asset, it does not apply because of the limited partnership. The reason for this would require a more complete examination of the partnership provisions of the tax laws, but in the final analysis the reason is that, to prevent abuse, it is not necessary to have more than the first rule apply. Accordingly, since the at risk rule applies to investments in all assets starting in 1979, the partnership at risk rule is no longer necessary and has been repealed. Starting in 1979, the at risk rule simply applies to all investments by individuals or partnerships, except in real estate.

These are the major tax-sheltering concepts, and the major limitations on them. Look for artificial losses, investment tax credits, and ways to convert ordinary income into capital gain. Look out for the limitations on interest deductions, at risk rules, recapture of investment tax credits and accelerated depreciation, and the minimum tax. Obviously, I have not covered all the ins and outs of tax shelters. There are as many variations of tax shelters as there are imaginative investors. There are also as many special rules as there are variations of tax shelters. But you should have a basic understanding of how tax shelters work. That does not mean that you should rely on your basic understanding to go out and invest in a tax shelter. These are complicated transactions, both in terms of financial concepts and tax concepts, and your investment plans should always be reviewed by people with extensive knowledge in both areas.

FIFTEEN
The Bottom Line

We started our tour through the tax laws by asking, "What is income?" We saw that everything is income unless the Code says it is not. In most of the rest of the book, we looked at what is not income or at what makes income less income.

This book has not made you a tax expert and it was not intended to. By reading it, you have had a basic law-school course in the income tax. Not as thorough a course as you find in law school, but an introduction to much of the material to which a prospective lawyer is exposed.

Students of a tax-law course do not become experts by the end of it. They take the tools given to them and they go from there. They understand what the basic law is, where it comes from, how it works and why. It is hoped that you understand these things too.

Sometimes as you come to understand the tax laws you begin to have strong feelings about them—one way or the other. I have tried to avoid passing my own judgment. The reasons for the laws which I have supplied are the official justifications (or at least my understanding of the official justifications)—the reasons Congress *claims* to have used in writing the laws and in making them so complex. Of course Congress can come up with a reason for anything. It just has to say, "This is the reason," and the law makes it so. Whether the reasons are valid, whether the law makes sense, whether its complexity is justifiable, whether it should encourage the activities it does encourage or whether it should be radically reformed—well, that is for you to decide. The book is intended only to help you make an intelligent decision.

You have come through some difficult material. The chapters on tax shelters, in particular, deal with complex tax law and sophisticated tax-law concepts.

If you feel you have a decent grasp of tax shelters, then you have a better understanding of the tax laws than you thought—because it is all there in tax shelters. If you still feel shaky about tax shelters, well, that shouldn't bother you either. Most people do. The reason some of us seem more conversant in these matters is that we look at them again and again. And each time that we come back, we are still uncertain.

If you are uncertain about tax shelters, or about any other parts of the tax law that we have discussed, you might read through parts of the book one more time. I say that fully aware of the risk of appearing presumptuous, but I say it based on some experience, because I have never found a tax law—never, not once—which I fully understood the first time around.

Index

Property damage, 75, 86–91
Property loss, 75
Property tax, 85–86
"Public policy," 140–141

Real estate rentals, "basis,"
175–176; depreciation of,
176–178, 184, 194–196, 202,
203, 218–219; improvement
of, 178–182, 183; interest deduction limits, 216–218;
recapturing depreciation,
214–216; as tax shelter, 183–
184, 193–196, 203; tax shelter
compared with equipment
leasing, 197–210; vacation-
home deduction, 143–150
Real estate taxes, 85–86, 94
"Real gain," 203
Real property, *see* Real estate
Recapture of depreciation,
214–216
Reimbursed business expenses,
46, 58
Religious leaders, 31
Retirement account, 71–72,
187, 190–191

Sales tax, 85–86
"Salvage value," 145
Scholarships, 36–40
Senior citizens, 14–16, 127
Sheltering income, *see* Tax
shelters
Short-term capital gains, 158–
165
Single taxpayer, 105, 109–110,
111–112

Social security taxes, 122
Solar equipment, and tax
credit, 126
Standard deduction, 44, 48, 74
State taxes, 75, 85–86
Stock dividends, 40
"Straight-line depreciation,"
145, 199
Syndicate, 225–228

Tables, tax, 115
Tax-avoidance, 112–113
Tax bracket, 77–79
Tax charts, 105–106
Tax credits, 8, 43, 75, 103, 121–
128; child-care, 123–125;
"foreign tax credit," 127;
"general tax credit," 127;
home insulation, 125–126;
investment tax credit, 127–
128; for low income, 127; miscellaneous, 122; political contributions, 122–123; for senior citizens, 127; tuition, 126–
127
Tax-free bonds, 188–190
Tax-free income, 23–41; and
armed forces, 29–31; and
clergy, 31; gifts, 31–33; from
health insurance company,
26–29; life insurance proceeds, 24–26; scholarships,
36–40
Tax liability, 8, 105–119; community property vs. common
law, 106–109; heads of
households, 110–111; income
averaging, 116–119; mar-